Secret Baggage
From Bondage to Freedom

[signature]

John 10:10

By Barry Bandara

Learn more about this book
and its author by visiting our website:
www.overboardministries.com

Copyright © 2021 Overboard Ministries
All rights reserved.
ISBN-13: 978-1-943635-32-0

This book is also available as an eBook.
Visit www.overboardministries.com for details.

Dedication

I dedicate this book to all those who call me "pastor" at GracePoint Church. I am honored to share my life and love with you all. A special dedication goes to those of you who were willing to share your story with me and the readers of this book. Thank you. May God use your stories to help someone find freedom from the bondage that comes from carrying baggage.

I also want to thank my parents, Barry and Georgene Bandara, for parenting me and my six siblings in such a way that limited the amount of baggage we carried into our marriages. We are forever indebted to you both.

Contents

Introduction

Sometimes I have a difficult time falling asleep on Saturday nights—especially when I am thinking about the sermon I am preparing to preach the next morning. The longer I go through the mental gymnastics of my message the more awake I become. Years ago, I found a solution to help me to fall asleep. It's a sleeping solution that I'm not sure a pastor, like myself, should share. But here it is: I listen to sermons from other pastors. I play someone speaking, I stop thinking about *my* message, and then fall asleep listening to *his*.

One late night in 2012, I started listening to Louie Giglio. He is the well-known and highly-gifted pastor of Passion City Church in Atlanta. Within minutes I knew I would not be falling asleep any time soon. I was gripped by the emotion and soberness I could clearly sense through my headphones. The message was so powerful that I knew God had directed me to listen to this sermon for a unique reason He would use later down the road. A year later, Louie's single sermon on the baggage people refuse to deal with became the inspiration for a five-week sermon series at GracePoint Church, where I serve. It was called *Secret Baggage*. It was a teaching series that I had never before nor since experienced in over thirty years as a pastor. Let me explain.

For those five weeks, I used a prop to unveil the issue we were going to address that morning. It was a well-worn five-drawer dresser. Each drawer had pieces of clothes peeking out around the corners to give the appearance that they were crammed full of clothes. Every week, after setting up the premise of the series, I would slowly open a drawer and pull out a simple sign that stated the name of the baggage for that day. Each time the sign became visible, I could sense the oxygen leaving the room. As a communicator you have those moments now and then, when you immediately realize a nerve has just been hit. In those moments you pause and think to yourself, "Slow down. Speak clearly. This is going to be difficult for someone to hear." And it was.

Occasionally, there are individuals who are moved to tears during a sermon. It could be due to the kind of week they have had, a current relationship crisis, or something God is convicting them about. Sometimes the tears flowing are completely unrelated to what you are teaching. It happens; not all the time, but it happens. What I did not expect on the first week of *Secret Baggage* was to witness many people, both

SECRET BAGGAGE IN YOUR LIFE WILL ROB YOU OF THE LIFE OF FREEDOM THAT GOD WANTS FOR YOU.

men and women, crying so early on in the message. It startled me to witness what was happening all around the auditorium and up into our balcony. To my added surprise, it continued throughout the entirety of the message, in all three services. The next Sunday arrived and the same thing happened again, but with different people emotionally moved. More tears, all throughout the message, at all three services.

Before the third Sunday in the series, several people asked me if I could tell them in advance what was going to be revealed from the next dresser drawer. They were hesitant about coming, or at least wanted to be emotionally prepared before they arrived. On that Sunday I acknowledged what was happening in our midst, and this became the first teaching series I could not wait to finish. It grieved me to see so many hurting people.

By the end of the five weeks, I had received numerous comments, emails, and Facebook messages of ways this series had impacted people's lives. Many jokingly asked "how I knew," or "Who told you?" It was not me at all. It was God. What I did not know during that sleepless night the year before was how many men and women in our church needed to be freed from the bondage of their baggage. Thankfully many started facing, for the first time, what had been stuffed in the corners of their life for so many years.

God Loves Us!
God loves us more than we realize; so much so that God sent His Son, Jesus, to come to earth to die in our place, for our sins. His death and resurrection purchased our spiritual freedom for all who believe. Jesus not only wants us to be spiritually free, but to be free in every area of our lives. As John 10:10 so aptly says, "The thief comes only to

steal and kill and destroy; I have come that they may have life, and have it to the full" (NIV).

Secret baggage in your life will rob you of the life of freedom that God wants for you. Satan, the thief mentioned in John 10:10, wants just the opposite. He wants to steal, kill, and destroy your joy, peace, hope, friendships, marriage, future, and more. Unresolved baggage will do this to you. Don't help this enemy by continuing to avoid unresolved issues in your life.

Fine Print Declaration
Just to be clear, I am not a counselor, nor do I play one on TV. But I am a pastor who loves people, and I have a passion and desire to help. Many of the baggage issues in this book are difficult. Some of them are extremely difficult. What I write in the following pages may hit a covered-up nerve that triggers a variety of emotions within you. If this is the case, you may very well need the help of a counselor that goes beyond my expertise and pay grade. If so, I highly encourage you to seek a Christian counselor who can provide you the kind of deep help you need, so that you can cross the line of both freedom and health. Don't hesitate.

Thankfully, if you are a believer in Jesus Christ, you have a Counselor available to you at all times. He is the Holy Spirit who Jesus promised His followers. Listen to Him. Obey Him, no matter how difficult.

If you truly want to move forward and experience a life of freedom, you will need to know three things up front:

- One, it will not be easy. Many times we can't see in the mirror what other people can see so clearly. Humility to face what you do not want to face is not easy. In fact, it can be painful. You may be tempted to throw this book across the room in anger. If it helps, throw it. Then, go pick it up and continue reading.

- Two, it will not be quick. Deep-seated baggage will take time to unseat in your mind, heart, and soul. Satan has most likely gained a foothold in your life and he will fight you tooth and nail to keep you in bondage. The fight for your freedom will not be easy.

- Three, it will be incredibly worth it. Anything of lasting worth is worth going after. Think about it: Jesus died on the cross for your freedom. He went willingly to the cross because he believed your freedom was worth it. So, hang in there and pursue wholeheartedly your freedom from the bondage from your baggage. You will be glad you did. You will read testimonies in most of the chapters from those who would verify the difficulty, and worth, of their freedom.

I trust that this book will help you on your journey to a life of freedom. If it does, please email me and tell me your story. I would love to hear from you and celebrate with you. If, while you are reading a chapter, someone comes to mind who is dealing with that particular baggage, send them their own copy as your way of helping and maybe even blessing them.

Chapter One

Backpack or U-Haul Trailer?

Our August wedding day finally arrived, and everything was ready. My bride, Candy, was inside the church making her final preparations with her bridesmaids as I waited outside, decked out in my pristine white tuxedo with long tails, pacing back and forth in excited anticipation. Hey, don't laugh; white tuxedos with tails were actually cool in 1985. However, that summer day was anything but cool. The temperature was in the mid-90s and the little church had neither airflow nor air conditioning. What could go wrong? Plenty.

I should have known our wedding ceremony was going to run long, given the fact that Candy's father and Papa were both pastors. While she stood linked to her father's arm in the center aisle, Papa opened the ceremony by telling many cute stories of his granddaughter growing up. Twenty minutes later, Candy and I finally made it onto the stage as her father took over the rest of the ceremony. He then started down his list of ten important principles for marital success. As the minutes passed, sweat began trickling down my back. I noticed that all the candles were beginning to cave and would soon collapse as they melted in the sweltering sauna of a church.

Just then I heard a loud boom, a brief pause, and then an even louder crash. The boom was from my brother Bobby's foot slamming into the floor as he desperately tried to regain his balance. It didn't help. The crash was his whole body hitting the floor, out cold. Another groomsman immediately swooped Bobby up and rushed him out of the room. Then Candy's little sister, Monique, started crying as this whole scene had scared her. As she was carried out, my baby brother, Bradley, finally noticed the many large, round, hanging ceiling lights, which prompted him to start yelling loudly, "Ball!" "Ball!"

Thankfully, Candy's father ditched the final six points of his marital challenge and wrapped it up, allowing us to gather downstairs for the reception in a much cooler room. But the surprises were not finished. As Candy and I prepared to leave for our honeymoon, we were told that everyone would be tossing small amounts of birdseed on us, instead of rice, for environmental reasons. We didn't know two teenage boys were on the roof with two large bags of birdseed. Just as we walked out, they poured both bags on top of our heads. When we finally arrived to our getaway car, I discovered a plywood wall had been inserted between the seats, making it impossible to see each other. By then, I was exasperated. I looked at my six-foot-five-inch Best Man and said, "Eric! Fix this!" He did, with several quick right-hand punches, and we were finally off.

SHOULD I DRIVE UP IN A COMPACT CAR OR RENT A U-HAUL TRAILER?

Although Candy and I were picking birdseed out of our hair for the next three days, we enjoyed our honeymoon. But just as there were unexpected surprises at our wedding, it did not take long to find more surprises waiting for us. Some surprises were the kind every marriage experiences, and some surprises were uniquely designed just for us.

Better Questions
Before the question of "Will you marry me?" is asked, and long before an answer to this question is given, I believe two better questions need to be asked. In fact, I believe these two questions should be asked before you ever start dating someone. Why? These two questions will help answer so many issues that will eventually come up in your lives together. If asked, these two questions will save much frustration, grief, tears, and confusion in life. They are: *"How much stuff do really you have?"* and, *"Should I drive up in a compact car or rent a U-Haul trailer?"*

We all have "stuff" we drag with us everywhere. It is the baggage we have collected throughout our life. This baggage is relational, emotional, financial, and generational. We all have baggage, every single one of us. It is the result of living in this sin-cursed world. But the choice we have is determining the size of baggage we choose to carry around. We could choose to carry a backpack of baggage, or choose to drive our baggage around in a U-Haul trailer. It does not feel like we have a choice, but it truly is our choice.

I call it Secret Baggage. We often go through life trying to hide our baggage in the dark closets of our lives, concealing it in the drawers of our relationships, deflecting it with personality and humor, or burying it with work and career. But over time, those who get close enough can figure out we have unresolved issues. Through our reactions, moodiness, tripped emotional responses, or erected walls of protection, people in our lives begin seeing the piles of baggage stuffed in the corners of our lives and notice the cluttered laundry seeping out of our metaphorical drawers. Baggage leads to bondage. Bondage breaks our spirit. Our spirit needs to be set free.

The First Step: Recognize There is a Problem

It is an age-old adage but nonetheless true: the first step to recovery is recognizing we have a problem and are powerless to fix it ourselves. I use the word "recovery" because we can tend to become addicted to our own baggage without even knowing it. Over time, baggage can become a close friend to us because we are with it all the time. It can even become who we think we are. But in order to be set free from the bondage of baggage, we must seek help beyond ourselves. There is a powerful story of moving from bondage to eventual freedom found in 2 Kings 5 that can help us.

> Now Naaman was commander of the army of the king of Aram. He was a great man in the sight of his master and highly regarded, because through him the Lord had given victory to Aram. He was a valiant soldier, but... (2 Kings 5:1)

Naaman appeared to have it all. Look at all the words communicating his success: *commander, great, victory, highly regarded,* and *valiant.* Naaman was an outstanding leader who was highly respected by many because of his courage when fighting battles. However, one little word changes his entire profile: *but.* He was a commander, *but.* He was great, *but.* He was victorious, *but.* He was highly regarded, *but.* He was valiant, *but.* That is a lot of "buts."

Depending on when we see someone and the setting in which we see them, we are often more acquainted with people's victories than their vulnerabilities. *Where* we see someone frequently determines *what* we see about them. And the same goes for us. It takes time to get to know the real person. It is one thing to be seen in the glow of positive press clippings, influence, and success. It is another thing to be seen under the harsh fluorescent lights of the trials of life. I have grown to distrust my first impressions of people. Too many times I have come to the wrong conclusions only to be disappointed or shocked later, because I often see what people *want* me to see. It is easy to assume that someone who acts bright, happy, and fun is just that. Then I find out they are anything but what they project. Others might seem boring but in reality they are not boring at all. They just do not go around causing massive drama for everyone around them. I have learned that drama works great in movies, but in everyday life I don't really want to purchase a ticket for that show.

The rest of the passage in 2 Kings 5 reveals the backstory on Naaman's life. Beyond the acclaim and awards, only a few people knew Naaman had the most dreaded disease known at that time: *"He was a valiant soldier, but he had leprosy."* What started out looking like dry skin in need of moisturizer would eventually become a nerve-killing, flesh-eating death warrant. Nobody on the battlefield would know there was a problem because on the battlefield he was covered up with armor. Armor, however, must eventually come off.

WE MAY IMPRESS PEOPLE FOR A WHILE, BUT EVENTUALLY THEY COME TO KNOW WE HAVE DAMAGING, UNRESOLVED ISSUES IN OUR LIVES. THE ARMOR OF PERSONALITY, HUMOR, GOOD LOOKS, AND SUCCESS WILL EVENTUALLY COME OFF.

So it is with secret baggage. We may impress people for a while, but eventually they come to know we have damaging, unresolved issues in our lives. The armor of personality, humor, good looks, and success will eventually come off. We can mislead people for a time, but only for a time. We may have a treasure trove of victories but our vulnerabilities will eventually overshadow any victory if our secret baggage is not addressed.

The Hard Step: Facing Fear

Now bands of raiders from Aram had gone out and had taken captive a young girl from Israel, and she served Naaman's wife. She said to her mistress, "If only my master would see the prophet who is in Samaria! He would cure him of his leprosy." (2 Kings 5:2-3)

Fear is one of the main reasons unresolved baggage remains unresolved. It is scary facing what we have chosen for so long to ignore. Most of us do not want to go through the necessary pain of confronting the baggage that we have long shoved away. When we are finally ready, all kinds of questions surface: *What will happen if I unpack certain baggage? How will I have to deal with it? How will other people react? Won't it be easier and better if I just leave things alone?*

I am sure Naaman faced all kinds of fears when he heard this little slave girl talking about his leprosy. *How many people now know about this? Does the king know? If he does, will I lose my career? How soon will my own family shun me or forcibly remove me?*

These types of fearful questions are normal and to be expected. Fear is a very real force in our world, and one of Satan's favorite tools to keep us in bondage. We will talk more about fear later in this book, but sticking our heads in the sand because of fear will never put us on the path to freedom. The only way fear works in our favor is when we become more fearful of what will happen if we do not do anything. Naaman's choice was stark: do nothing and die. "Naaman went to his master and told him what the girl from Israel had said. 'By all means, go,' the king of Aram replied" (2 Kings 5:4-5).

The Biggest Step: Choosing Humility
In addition to fear, pride is another reason unresolved baggage remains unresolved. Seeking help is humbling. Forgiving someone who hurt us is humbling. Admitting failure is humbling. Looking face-to-face at our own ugliness is humbling. Asking others to forgive us is, yes, humbling. Such is freedom: never easy or free, but well worth it.

Thankfully, this great warrior took some great advice from a little girl; a slave girl at that, and from an enemy nation. Naaman's character is revealed in that he listened to someone who was inferior to him. Once his disease was exposed he could have punished her for speaking up, but instead he went to his king and asked permission to seek help from the prophet of their enemy. His character passed the first test. It would be tested more severely in short order.

How do you react when some of your baggage is exposed? When your well-guarded armor is missing, maybe you have a meltdown at work, an emotional outburst toward your teenager, a cursed-filled response in anger, or an unexplained wall going up with someone you love. When confronted with your actions, how do you react? Do you blow it off? Justify it? Deny it? Get defensive? Your reaction will be a good indicator of the integrity of your character and the true measure of your emotional health. Naaman passed the initial step of humility by seeking help, but then failed when receiving it.

> So Naaman went with his horses and chariots and stopped at the door of Elisha's house. Elisha sent a messenger to say to him, "Go, wash yourself seven times in the Jordan and your flesh will be restored and you will be cleansed." But Naaman went away angry. (2 Kings 5:9-11a)

First, Naaman was offended that the prophet did not come to greet him but sent a servant instead. *Don't you know who I am? Don't disrespect me!* Later, he was appalled when told to wash in the dirty Jordan River instead of the clean rivers back at home. *Don't make me do that! My way is a much better way!* In his anger, Naaman started to head home. Thankfully, Naaman rightly responded when confronted —again—by his *servant* who said, in the ancient "Bandara" translation, *"Dude! Get a grip! If you had been told to do something great, you would have done it. Just do what Elisha told you to do!"* And he did. "So he went down and dipped himself in the Jordan seven times, as the man of God had told him, and his flesh was restored and became clean like that of a young boy" (2 Kings 5:14).

An Important Step: Seeking the Right Help

I jumped over an important part of this passage that is critical in finding freedom for unresolved baggage in our life: it is imperative that we seek not just any help, but the right kind of help. Naaman's story almost made a tragic turn right out of the gate after his king gave him permission to travel to Israel for help. See if you can catch his mistake in this passage:

> So Naaman left, taking with him ten talents of silver, six thousand shekels of gold and ten sets of clothing. The letter that he took to the king of Israel read: "With this letter I am sending my servant Naaman to you so that you may cure him of his leprosy." (2 Kings 5:5b-6)

Sometimes our friends or love ones are well-intentioned but not entirely helpful in their attempts to relieve us of our unresolved baggage. Naaman's king asked the king of Israel to cure his commander. That is not who the little servant girl recommended. The king had no power to help; the prophet of God did. The king of Israel's response to this request revealed a glimpse of his own secret baggage.

> As soon as the king of Israel read the letter, he tore his robes and said, "Am I God? Can I kill and bring back to life? Why does this fellow send someone to me to be cured of his leprosy? See how he is trying to pick a quarrel with me!" (2 Kings 5:7)

Past attacks can trigger present defensive reactions. These kinds of triggers can move us into overreactions at the speed of light. Thankfully, Elisha heard of this request and told the king to send Naaman down to his house.

Seeking the right help is important. You must seek God's truth as your source for help. There are plenty of self-help books comprised of man's wisdom and void of God's power. **LASTING FREEDOM FROM OUR SECRET BAGGAGE IS ONLY POSSIBLE WITH DIVINE INTERVENTION.** In each chapter of this book I have tried to provide you with biblical truth from God's Word to help you with whatever baggage you have accumulated. The answers and help are not from me but from God's truth.

There also comes a time when everyone needs to see a counselor to dig deep into what is going on beneath the surface. I fully anticipate this book can begin the healing process, but you might need a good counselor to help you cross the finish line of freedom. My advice: seek a counselor that can offer you healthy and biblical counsel for what you are facing.

Several years ago I was extremely unhealthy. Years of pastoral ministry had worn me down. Several of my church staff recommended that I see a counselor, but I was not ready to do so. Months later, my safely guarded armor fell off and I reacted on social media to a critical comment. Before I responded, there was a small still voice telling me,

"Don't post this! Don't send it! Delete it!" I didn't listen. I sent it and felt justified—briefly. Within a minute I received a private message from my good friend and pastoral assistant, Lindsay. She lovingly but directly confronted me on what I wrote. As Proverb 27:6 says, "Faithful are the wounds of a friend." What Lindsay said hurt, because it was true. She was faithful to give me what I needed to hear.

I said nothing to my wife, out of shame, and headed quietly upstairs. I went into our bathroom and looked intently into the mirror. What I saw grabbed my attention like never before. I saw a bitter, angry, and hurting man. I clearly remember thinking to myself, *"I do not recognize this man in the mirror, but I refuse to be him!"* Right then and there I determined that I would call a counselor first thing in the morning.

That next morning I took the steps I just outlined for you: I recognized I had a problem, faced my fear, chose humility, and sought the right kind of help. A year later, I was finally healthy and no longer in bondage. I pray this book will help you on your own journey to freedom.

Chapter Two
Generational Sin

Let me tell you a true story. Years ago, at a lake located in the high desert an hour east of Bakersfield, California, a lady was having a hard time with her brand new twenty-two-foot Bayliner ski boat. New to boating, she just couldn't understand why her boat would not perform, no matter how hard she tried. Even when she had the throttle opened up all the way, it would not balance at all and was sluggish in almost every maneuver. *"Either I just bought a lemon of a boat,"* she thought, *"or I am doing something wrong. This is not the way it's supposed to be!"*

After about an hour of trying to make it go, she motored over to a nearby marina. Maybe they could tell her what was wrong. Once she docked, she told one of the guys at the marina how the boat was performing and asked if he could help her by finding the problem. He immediately climbed into the boat and started a thorough topside check. Twenty minutes later he told her that everything was in perfect working order. The engine ran fine, the outdrive went up and down, the prop was the correct size and pitch. A little confused, he told her he could only think of one additional check. So, he jumped into the water to check underneath. Immediately, he came up choking on water, he was laughing so hard. (Remember, this is a true story.) Under the boat, still strapped securely in place, was the trailer.

The first baggage that we need to unpack is like the submerged trailer still attached to the boat: it is called *Generational Sin*. This baggage will be such a drag in your life, relationships, and family that you will continually wonder what is wrong and why everything seems so difficult. So what is generational sin? It is any sinful attitude, action, belief, behavior, or habit that we inherit from our parents. What I mean by inherit is this: they modeled for us or even encouraged in our presence certain attitudes, actions, beliefs, behaviors, or habits that are now a regular part of our life. What was theirs has, over time, become ours as well. If you do not deal with it you will pass the same baggage on to your children, who will most likely pass it on to their children. And on and on it goes. It is generational.

I have a newsflash for you: your parents are not perfect. News? Hardly.

Since the Garden of Eden, every single human being has been infected with the disease called sin. It started with Adam and Eve and has been passed on to every human being since. Sin is not a word our culture uses that often, so what is it? It is any thought, word, deed, or attitude that misses God's standard of perfection. We have all missed it, and we miss it all the time. God says in Romans 3:23, "For all have sinned and fall short of the glory of God." That is why Jesus came to Earth that very first Christmas. That is why He died on the cross and then rose from the grave, proving He had power over sin and death. Jesus was the only perfect sacrifice that could pay our sin debt and make us right with God.

When we choose to accept Jesus Christ as Savior, for who He is and what He did for our salvation, a huge transformation takes place. One, all of our sins are forgiven. Two, we are given the Holy Spirit to help guide us in every aspect of our daily life. And three, we now have access to divine power to change us from the inside out. I have seen transformational change over and over in the lives of people who have been set free by Christ. Drunks turn sober, addicts become clean, angry hearts soften, and the anxious grow calm. That is what God can do when we allow Him to turn our darkness to light.

While Jesus can immediately change our soul, the imprints our parents made on our lives do not disappear overnight. We often do not realize how much we are like our father or mother until we are older and catch ourselves talking, acting, and responding just like they did. It can be uncomfortable when it hits us that we are more like one or both of our parents than we have realized.

Crazy Sin Cycle
King David is a biblical rock star. He was a God follower, giant killer, conquering warrior, successful king, and creative songwriter. He succeeded in every area of life, except as a father. He failed miserably

because he failed to deal with the secret baggage in his life. But in the confines of his home he had a bunch of little boys and girls who watched him model bad habits and bad decisions. Some baggage David never addressed. Others he tried to cover up. And David's baggage eventually became his children's baggage. When his son, Solomon, was on the throne, he took the baggage his father gave him and multiplied it. He took what David did and did it in excess. What David passed on to Solomon, Solomon passed on to his kids. And on it went: generational sin.

Solomon's generational sin was so bad that God said to him,

> Since this is your attitude and you have not kept my covenant and my decrees, which I commanded you, I will most certainly tear the kingdom away from you and give it to one of your subordinates. (1 Kings 11:11)

When Solomon died, his son Rehoboam replaced him as king. Shortly after Rehoboam became king of the nation of Israel, God ripped the majority of the kingdom away from him. God left him with only two tribes out of the twelve. After Rehoboam died, many kings who succeeded him did not follow after God. The nation continued to sin and God continue to punish the nation for their sins. Generational sin continued.

The ten other tribes went with a man called Jeroboam, who was one of Solomon's council members. God promised Jeroboam if he would follow God like David did, he would be blessed like God blessed David. What an incredible opportunity—yet Jeroboam ignored God completely. He even fashioned two golden calves, and said, "These are the gods that brought us out of Egypt" (1 Kings 12:28). Jeroboam sounded just like Aaron and did what Aaron did in Exodus 32. I mean, how crazy could you be? There were seventeen kings of the northern tribes that followed after Jeroboam. Scripture says time and time again that king after king *"did not turn away from the sins of Jeroboam."* What a pathetic generational legacy. God finally gave a final warning in 2 Kings 17.

> Do not forget the covenant I have made with you and do not worship other gods. Rather, worship the Lord your God; it is

He who will deliver you from the hand of all your enemies. (2 Kings 17:38-39)

Here is what happened:

They would not listen, however, but persisted in their former practices. Even while these people were worshiping the Lord, they were serving their idols. To this day their children and grandchildren continue to do as their fathers did. (2 Kings 17:40-41)

They continued to sin as their fathers did: generational sin. God had to respond and, when He did, it was severe. God allowed the Assyrians to conquer the northern kingdom and take them off into captivity. This part of David's nation dispersed, disappeared, and never returned.

Changing the Cycle

The cycle of generational sin can stop. It can change. In fact, the cycle of generational sin can completely turn around and become a new cycle of generational blessing. In chapter 18 of 2 Kings, we see the cycle of generational sin broken by a man named Hezekiah. Before I tell you about him, let me give you the story of Hezekiah's family. His great-grandfather, Uzziah, passionately sought the Lord and followed Him for most of his life. When Uzziah died, his son, Jotham, became king and followed God —more or less. 2 Chronicles says, "[Jotham] did what was right in the eyes of the Lord, just as his father Uzziah had done, but unlike him he did not enter the temple of the Lord" (2 Chronicles 27:2).

THE CYCLE OF GENERATIONAL SIN CAN COMPLETELY TURN AROUND AND BECOME A NEW CYCLE OF GENERATIONAL BLESSING.

2 Kings 15 paints a picture of Jotham walking the fence of truly following after God. He liked God but would not worship Him in the temple. He did some good things, but he also allowed evil practices to continue. He did what was right in the eyes of God but allowed his people to do what was evil in the sight of God. Jotham was a lukewarm follower of God. Then Jotham passed his kingdom to his son, Ahaz, who was the father of Hezekiah. The progression went like

this: a great-grandfather who was a red-hot follower of God, to a grandfather who was a lukewarm follower of God, to Hezekiah's father who was an ice-cold, evil, absolutely without-a-doubt non-follower of God.

Hezekiah grew up with a father who took the gold and silver from the temple of the Lord and gave it to the heathen king of Assyria as a payoff bribe. Hezekiah watched his father take one of his brothers and offer him up as a human sacrifice in a sadistic pagan worship service. Yes, he killed his son in worship to some idol! This is the role model, example, and pattern that Hezekiah witnessed in his youth. I doubt that you had it this rough growing up. You may have had a poor role model with one or even both parents, but you most likely never lost a sibling the way Hezekiah did. Would Hezekiah follow in the footsteps of his father or would he break the cycle of generational sin?

> Hezekiah did what was right in the eyes of the Lord, just as his father David had done. He removed the high places, smashed the sacred stones and cut down the Asherah poles. He broke into pieces the bronze snake Moses had made, for up to that time the Israelites had been burning incense to it. Hezekiah trusted in the Lord, the God of Israel. There was no one like him among all the kings of Judah, either before him or after him. He held fast to the Lord and did not stop following him. He kept the commands the Lord had given Moses. (2 Kings 18:3-6)

Hezekiah made a choice that changed his life and his nation. In obedience to God, Hezekiah destroyed the many places of idolatrous worship that involved all kinds of sick, sexual prostitution disguised as worship. He even demolished something that started out as a good thing during the time of Moses but had become another idol of pagan worship. Hezekiah was bold, courageous, serious, and determined to not only say he was a follower of

HOW BADLY DO YOU TRULY WANT GOD'S BLESSING IN YOUR LIFE, YOUR FAMILY, AND YOUR FINANCES?

God but, by his actions, show that he truly followed and trusted God. Not only did Hezekiah break the cycle of generational sin he was raised with, he experienced the blessings of God as a result. How would you like this following statement to be said about you? "And the Lord was with him; he was successful in whatever he undertook" (2 Kings 18:7).

I don't know about you, but I want God's blessing in my life—not just a little blessing but blessings that are overflowing. How badly do you truly want God's blessing in your life, your family, and your finances? But have you determined to follow after God with all of your heart? I'll ask it again for effect: How badly do you want God's blessing in your life? Hezekiah wanted it badly, and with his actions he made some hard choices. As a result, God blessed him. In doing so, Hezekiah broke the cycle of generational sin.

Now, I am pretty confident that you do not have an evil, pagan worship shrine in your garage or backyard, where you sacrifice children and have a weird, sexual kind of worship. (If you do, don't tell me, because if you do I am going to call the police.) But every one of us suffers from generational sin that has passed from one generation to the next. If we are honest, we are loading up our children with baggage that was modeled for us, and that we are modeling now. We were encouraged to pick up this baggage, and we are encouraging our kids to pick it up even though we are not saying the words. This generational sin was never dealt with in your parent's life, and you have never dealt with it. Here are some examples of generational sins.

Worry
Some of you had moms who were "worry warts" who would worry, worry, worry, worry, worry, worry, get stressed, be tense, get stressed, be tense, and worry, worry, worry, some more. They worried about everything. When you were growing up your mother was so protective of you that she put kneepads, shoulder pads, helmets, and padding everywhere so you would never get a scratch. Then you became a teenager, and her worrying became the completely-freaking-out kind of worry. She started asking questions that good parents need to ask, such as, "Where are you going? Who's going to be there? When are you going to come back?" But your mother did not ask those questions just for information. She asked so she could go to her worry, worry, worry world. What she was really thinking was, *"You have to call me when you get there so that I'll know you're not dead on the side of the road. As a matter of fact, I wish you would call me at every stoplight, so I'll know that you got through the light.*

And then when you arrive, please call me again and let me know if there is a police car nearby in case of emergency!"

I am exaggerating to make my point, but with some of you it is not much of a stretch. You probably grew up thinking, *"My mom's a worry freak. She's crazy. I will never ever be like her."* But now you are older, and you have children. And in your home, every wall has a corner bumper piece. Every cabinet door is locked, because your children could drink something dangerous and die. You're stressed, and you are always worrying. As your children become teenagers, you ask all the crazy questions your mother asked. *"Where are you going? Who are you going with? When are you going to be back? Has everyone there had his or her flu shot? Call me. Call me. Call me. Call me!"* You call it being a responsible parent but it is much more than this; it is stress and worry. If you are honest, you should look in the mirror and say, *"Hello, Mom. It's great to see you again."* Why do you act like that? It is because you were taught to act this way. It was modeled for you.

Worry is, in fact, a sin. When we worry, we are telling God that He cannot handle what we are worrying about. It is impossible to trust God and worry at the same time. Too many of us have become experts at condoning worry as a low-level sin that God does not really care about. In fact, to worry is to fear and we are commanded in Scripture, time and again, not to fear. It is like God telling us, *"Don't worry. Trust me instead."*

Anger
Some of you grew up with an angry father. It seemed like he was angry all the time. He was stressed, tense, and wound up so tight and so often that you were stressed, tense, and wound up when you heard him coming home after work. You would immediately think, *"I hope he had a good day at work. I hope, I hope he had a good day!"* Deep down inside of you was a sigh of sheer relief if he came home in a good mood. However, you were still a little on edge the rest of the night because you prayed nothing would happen to change his good mood.

Oh, how you dreaded the days when he came home upset. You could hear it in his footsteps when he walked inside. The whole house seemed filled with tension because something happened at work, or someone responded the wrong way to him, or cut him off while driving home. Whatever set him off was now going to be taken out against everyone at home. His hurtful words, angry tone, and painful comments cut like a knife. As much as you tried to avoid him and hide away in your room, you could still feel and even hear his anger echoing throughout the house. But it was always worse when you did something to make him angry. A simple accident or an innocent comment he did not appreciate would cause him to blow up. You cringed so hard it hurt. Part of you seemed to die whenever this happened. You remember a growing anger inside of you whenever your father yelled at you in a completely disrespectful way for being disrespectful to him.

Deep down in the crevices of your soul you vowed that you would never, ever be like your father. You would never treat your kids the way he treated you. You would never talk to those you love the way he did. You would never marry someone like him. You grew to lose all respect for him. You hated how he acted. Maybe you even hated him.

But now you are older, with all the pressures of life and the financial weight that comes with having a family. You are stressed. You are tense. Your fuse is short. And everyone has learned to walk on eggshells when you come around, not knowing what kind of mood you are in. They are hoping and praying that you have had a good day; wishing upon a star that you are not angry. Again. And if you are honest, you should look in the mirror and say, "Hello, Dad. I didn't want you to live here. But you do." So why do you act like this? Why do you respond this way? It is because you were taught to. It was modeled for you.

Being angry is not actually a sin. Ephesians 4:26 states, "In your anger do not sin." It is what we do when we are angry that make all the difference. Yelling, cursing, throwing things, slamming doors, and getting physical when we are angry is a sin. It damages. It destroys. It scars, for life. This generational sin needs to stop.

There's More

Some of you have been unfaithful to your spouse—just like one of your parents was unfaithful. Some of you are financially irresponsible. You learned it well. Some of you vowed you would never drink alcohol because of the stain of an alcoholic you lived with. Now loved ones are telling you that you drink too much. Some of you hedge the truth because the truth was always hedged at home. Some of you are prideful and arrogant. You can see a pattern of this in your past.

Then there is greed, laziness, unreliability, abuse, rejection, insecurity, pornography, resentment, emotional dependency, lack of self-control, manipulation, controlling tendencies, and on and on it goes. It is passed from one generation to the next generation. One day it dawns on you, like the woman with the trailer still strapped to her boat, *"Something is wrong. It's not supposed to be this way!"*

There Is Hope
No matter how well you might live, how beautiful you might appear, and how stunning your home may be, dysfunctional families beget dysfunction. Every home has some sort of dysfunction, even pastors' homes. All of us are affected by the sins of our parents. There is no denying this. But there truly is hope.

Not only is there hope for us to enjoy the freedom of being set free from the generational sin of our past, but we can also position our children with a better future that is free from our junk. We must realize,

ALL OF US ARE AFFECTED BY THE SINS OF OUR PARENTS. THERE IS NO DENYING THIS. BUT THERE TRULY IS HOPE.

however, that this hope cannot come from us. It is impossible. It's above our pay grade. This kind of hope can only come from God. To experience freedom from generational sin, here are some steps to take.

Step One: Trust in Christ
God has provided a path for our freedom, and it begins by having a personal relationship with God. It begins by being filled with God's power, which can break the cycle of generational sin. With His power at your disposal your life, attitude, response, and even bad habits can change.

Let this sink in: generational sin has no authority over a believer. If you are on the outside looking in with Christianity and Christ, and have not accepted Jesus as your Savior, I ache for you; without Christ we are hopeless. Yes, you can go to a counselor. Yes, you can take medication. Yes, you can busy yourself with a job and a career, trying to distract yourself from all your baggage. But without Jesus Christ we carry our baggage alone. We cannot unpack it or hide it or be set free from it. That is why you need to trust in Christ; Jesus changes everything. Again, generational sin has no authority over a believer. Paul writes,

> When you were dead in your sins and in the uncircumcision of your sinful nature, God made you alive with Christ. He forgave us all our sins, having cancelled the charge of our legal indebtedness, which stood against us and condemned us; He has taken it away, nailing it to the cross. (Colossians 2:13-14)

I do not like talking about circumcision. It is uncomfortable, to say the least. But Paul mentioned it first. Earlier in Colossians he described it this way, "In him you were also circumcised with a circumcision not performed by human hands. Your whole self ruled by the flesh was put off when you were circumcised by Christ" (Colossians 2:11).

What in the world is he saying? Paul is talking about a spiritual surgery that takes place the moment we trust in Jesus as Savior. Before salvation, we are attached to our sin nature. It is our master and we are its slave. As a result, we are magnetically pulled to all kinds of sin that our sinful nature calls out for and our flesh craves. But when we trust in Christ we are cut away (circumcised) from the power of our sinful nature. This is the first step toward freedom from generational sin.

Step Two: Refuse to Be a slave
President Abraham Lincoln issued the Emancipation Proclamation on January 1, 1863, as our nation began its third year of a bloody civil war. Lincoln declared "that all persons held as slaves," within the rebellious states, "are, and henceforward shall be free." Although this presidential proclamation did not end the Civil War, it was a vital tipping point in American history. It set in motion the long journey of removing the scourge of slavery, which had stained our country for too many years. Two years later, on December 6, 1865, the Thirteenth Amendment was passed, abolishing slavery in the United States once and for all. While we rejoice in the fact that slaves were given their freedom by this amendment, a substantial number of freed slaves stayed with their masters, some for a decade or longer. The primary

reason was that they did not have available resources to survive on their own. Their newfound freedom was, in many ways, useless to them.

Thankfully, at salvation the Holy Spirit is given to new believers, and He is our best resource for our new freedom in Christ. He teaches us, guides us, convicts us of sin, and helps us choose a new course of action in our lives. Before salvation we had little choice because we were slaves to our sin nature. After salvation, now we can choose whether or not to sin. We can choose to remain in slavery to our sin. On the other hand, we now have the ability, through Christ, to choose freedom from our sinful past. As a result, generational sin is no longer in control. In the book of Galatians, Paul pleads with us not to return to being slaves to our sin. "It is for freedom that Christ has set us free. Stand firm, then, and do not let yourselves be burdened again by a yoke of slavery" (Galatians 5:1).

Step Three: Follow the Spirit
Paul then appeals to us to follow the Spirit, resulting in drastic changes in our lives. Instead of listening to our sin nature, we listen to and follow the Spirit of God who is charting a new course in our lives. "Those who belong to Christ Jesus have crucified the sinful nature with its passions and desires. Since we live by the Spirit, let us keep in step with the Spirit" (Galatians 5:24-25).

Keeping in step with the Spirit sounds complicated but it is simply this: when the Spirit says *go*, you go. When He says *stop*, you stop. When He says, *do not open your mouth because you are going to say something inappropriate or stupid*, you do not open your mouth.

When we are keeping in step with the Spirit it manifests itself in our choices, attitudes, and responses when irritated. Instead of acting out your programmed generational sin, you are allowing the Holy Spirit to reprogram you to follow His leading. As a result, you will experience new kinds of fruit in your life: "But the fruit of the Spirit is love, joy, peace, forbearance, kindness, goodness, faithfulness, gentleness and self-control. Against such things there is no law" (Galatians 5:22-23).

The attitudes and actions of generational sin look nothing like this list. It is usually is the opposite. But with your newfound freedom in Christ and the best resource available to believers, the Holy Spirit, choosing to keep in step with the Spirit will slowly but surely change your future from generational sin to generational blessing.

Step Four: Fight for Your family!

Breaking the cycle of generational sin will not be easy. It may go more slowly than you would like but it will be worth it. Do not quit. Instead, fight! Yes, fight for the future of your family. Fight for your family to be delivered from the repeated sin that has crippled your past and present, and brought all sorts of pain and sorrow along with it. Your future is worth fighting for. Your children's future is worth fighting for. So, fight!

Nehemiah is famous in the Bible for leading the charge to rebuild the broken and torn-down walls around the ancient city of Jerusalem. Before he arrived to lead this campaign, he heard the people in and around the city were living "*in trouble*" and "*in disgrace.*" And it had been that way for generations. To them it was normal, but to Nehemiah it was unacceptable to continue living this way. So he challenged them in similar ways I am challenging you in this book. He said to the crowd,

YOUR FUTURE IS WORTH FIGHTING FOR. YOUR CHILDREN'S FUTURE IS WORTH FIGHTING FOR. SO, FIGHT!

> You see the trouble we are in: Jerusalem lies in ruins, and its gates have been burned with fire. Come, let us rebuild the wall of Jerusalem, and we will no longer be in disgrace. (Nehemiah 2:17)

The people grew excited, but their fervor to rebuild the wall and reclaim a new future for them and their families quickly faded. They were not prepared as they immediately faced ridicule, anger, discouragement, and internal strife. So here is what Nehemiah did:

> Then I stationed men in the lowest parts of the space behind the wall, the exposed places, and I stationed the people in families with their swords, spears and bows. When I saw their fear, I rose and spoke to the nobles, the officials and the rest of the people: "Do not be afraid of them; remember the Lord who is great and awesome, and fight for your brothers, your

sons, your daughters, your wives and your houses." (Nehemiah 4:13-14)

You may read this chapter, or this book for that matter, and get fired up with excitement and determination to get rid of certain baggage in your life. Finally, you are ready to address what has been ignored or justified for so long. But beware. It will not be easy, and you will not taste victory without a fight. So, fight!

Fight for your sons!
Fight for your daughters!
Fight for your wife!
Fight for your husband!
Fight for your family!
Fight for your future!

Generational sin can be conquered, defeated, and vanquished in your life and home. You can someday view your generational sin as a bad memory, left in your past. With God's help you can be victorious, and you and your family will begin new, positive, and healthy memories. These are the kind of memories that put a smile on your face instead of a pit in your gut. You can begin new habits that you would be proud to pass on to the next generation. You can have a new future of trusting instead of worrying, a future with self-control in your reactions, and integrity in your character that becomes the new legacy of your life. It can happen. Take one step at a time, but take each step in step with the Holy Spirit. Walk and live in freedom, without a boat trailer still strapped on and dragging underneath you.

Chapter Three

Enabling

My wife is a fantastic parent. Candy studied and learned the ways each of our three girls were uniquely different, and parented each of them accordingly. Without hesitation, she showed tender love when the girls needed it and rendered tough love whenever necessary. The one thing that Candy never did as a parent was enable any of our girls. She inspected what she expected on a consistent basis. Our girls learned they couldn't play the martyr or victim with their mother because it never worked. It was an exercise in futility to try manipulating their mom with emotion, drama, or excuses.

The way Candy treats our dog, Rusty, is entirely different story. She is consistently manipulated by his big brown eyes, wagging tail, and pathetic whine. What Candy never did with our daughters she regularly does with our four-legged pet: she gives in to his every wish. When Rusty first came to our home, at night Candy would pick him up to place him on her corner of the bed. Even though he can easily jump up on the bed himself, he figured out that the bat of his eyes and a little whine would cause Candy to pick him up.

We recently repurposed a sitting bench that now resides at the foot of our bed. With little effort, Rusty is able to jump up on the bench and step onto the bed. After I teased Candy about how much she has enabled Rusty, she determined not to pick him up. The first night she refused to place him on the bed, he began to wail loudly. We laughed at his wretchedness while his howling lasted for twenty minutes, until he jumped up on the bench, stepped onto our bed, and plopped down in his corner with an angry grunt. Why did he react this way? Because he had been conditioned to receive first-class bed service from my wife.

Enabling a pet can produce some minor inconveniences. Enabling a child, spouse, parent, or friend can result in great and lasting damage. Enabling is when we allow irresponsible behavior from someone we love, and then rescue him or her from any accountability or consequence they deserve.

On the surface, enabling is disguised as helping, caring, and loving. It sounds like, *"But I love them so much; I am just trying to help."* When irresponsible behavior is allowed to continue and when people choose to look the other way, enabling can be costly. It can even be deadly.

Enabling shows up when a parent withholds accountability and consequences for attitudes and actions that are completely inappropriate from their child. Because they do not want to face their child or confront them, or be viewed as the bad parent, they look the other way. Or the parent may loudly express how upset and disappointed they are, but then refuse to apply the much-needed punishment that was promised. Then, after a few hours or days, the parent somehow rationalizes that everything is okay because their child said the magic words, *"I'm sorry."* As a result, nothing happens. No accountability is applied. No consequence is felt. And more enabling ensues.

Parents are not the only ones who enable. Adult children can enable their adult parents, siblings can enable another sibling, a boss can enable his employees, friends can enable their friends, spouses can enable their spouse; it can happen in any relationship. When we allow irresponsible behavior and then try to rescue the guilty party or excuse, shield, and keep them from accountability and consequences, we may believe we are helping them but we are, in fact, hurting them.

WHEN WE ENABLE, OUR IRRESPONSIBILITY WILL EVENTUALLY BECOME SOMEONE ELSE'S RESPONSIBILITY.

In the end this leads to more problems, more repeated incidents, and more baggage that someone eventually has to clean up.

Being Irresponsible with Responsibility

Here is the hard truth: when we enable, our irresponsibility will eventually become someone else's responsibility. For example, if a parent is irresponsible with disciplining his or her child, someone will eventually become involved with correcting the bad behavior that was not corrected by the parent. In childhood it could be a coach, a school counselor, or a principal. In the future it could be a boss, a spouse, a policeman, or the warden at the prison. Someone else is forced to be responsible because someone was irresponsible with their responsibility. Tracing the damage will reveal clues that someone was enabled. Eventually, ignored consequences will result in greater consequences for a greater number of people down the road.

> ENABLING IS WHEN WE ALLOW IRRESPONSIBLE BEHAVIOR FROM SOMEONE WE LOVE, AND THEN RESCUE HIM OR HER FROM ANY ACCOUNTABILITY OR CONSEQUENCE THEY DESERVE.

Here Comes the Judge

Eli was the second-to-last judge in the Old Testament before the nation of Israel started having kings. Eli was also the High Priest. He was a godly man. He loved the Lord. Eli loved following and serving God. But he had two sons, Hophni and Phinehas, who were flat-out wicked. They had no regard for God, but for some crazy reason Eli allowed his two wicked sons to serve as priests underneath him. At that time priests, according to the Old Testament Law, were allowed a certain allotment of the food and offerings that were brought in by the people for their Torah-mandated sacrifice. But Hophni and Phinehas went well beyond their allotment. If they wanted extra meat offered to the priests, they took it. When they wanted extra cash in their wallets, they took it. These boys took whatever they wanted to take, whenever they wanted to take it.

Eli's sons had little regard for the people when they came to worship or make sacrifices to the Lord. Hophni and Phinehas were rude and harsh with them. They didn't care. They also violated God's morality laws and slept with women who assisted them in the Lord's work. Again, they didn't care. Here is how they are described in Scripture:

"Eli's sons were scoundrels; they had no regard for the Lord" (1 Samuel 2:12).

Everybody knew these guys were wicked, including their father Eli. The only thing Eli did was give his sons a warning, but nothing of real consequence.

> Now Eli, who was very old, heard about everything his sons were doing to all Israel and how they slept with the women who served at the entrance to the tent of meeting. So he said to them, "Why do you do such things? I hear from all the people about these wicked deeds of yours. No, my sons; the report I hear spreading among the Lord's people is not good. If one person sins against another, God may mediate for the offender; but if anyone sins against the Lord, who will intercede for them?" His sons, however, did not listen to their father's rebuke. (1 Samuel 2:22-25)

The time came when God had had enough and sent Eli the following message through the young priest-in-training named Samuel:

> And the LORD said to Samuel: "See, I am about to do something in Israel that will make the ears of everyone who hears about it tingle. At that time I will carry out against Eli everything I spoke against his family—from beginning to end. For I told him that I would judge his family forever because of the sin he knew about; his sons made themselves contemptible, and he failed to restrain them." (1 Samuel 3:11-13)

Everybody knew that Hophni and Phinehas were out of control, but Eli failed to do anything about it. He just picked up the rug and swept everything they did underneath it. He looked the other way. He did not confront them. He did not hold them accountable. He did not even remove them from them their positions as priests. He could have; he had the authority and the power. He just let it slide. He failed to restrain them. He enabled them. Finally, God rebuked Eli for it. "Why do you honor your sons more than me?" (2 Kings 2:29).

Ouch! I hope that none of us are guilty of the same, especially parents. But it happens all the time. When we enable, we end up honoring those we are enabling over God.

You see, when those little bundles of sin called babies come into our family, we love them so much. If we are not careful, we can easily place our children above God. The same is true with our children, grandchildren, spouse, or anyone important to us. We can end up being more concerned about them than we are about God. So, we shy away from taking actions that potentially could hurt or offend them. When we do this, God has the same question for us that He had for Eli, *"Why do you honor them more than me?"*

Eli was irresponsible with his responsibility to his sons. Therefore, God had to take responsibility for Eli's irresponsibility. This led to the early and tragic death of Hophni and Phinehas. Sadly, Eli's lasting legacy was of a father who enabled his sons … to their death.

King of Enabling
Years later the young prophet, Samuel, took over for Eli. He was the prophet who anointed a teenage shepherd boy to be the second king over the nation of Israel. After fifteen long and dangerous years, David ascended to the throne of Israel. David authentically loved God. He loved worshipping God. He was exceptionally skilled at writing worship songs about God. Some of his lyrics are still used in churches today. But David was irresponsible with his responsibility as a parent. Time and time again, when David needed to step up as a father, he punted.

When David's oldest son, Amnon, raped his stepsister Tamar, David was emotionally distressed but could not bring himself to punish his son. David's inaction caused his second son, Absalom, to take action that ultimately led to Amnon being ambushed and killed. Absalom's bitterness and hatred of his father eventually led him to attempt to overthrow David from his throne. His coup ultimately failed, costing Absalom his life. In fact, David continued to carry the consequences of his baggage of enablement to his deathbed. As he was dying, another son tried to usurp the throne from David's appointed heir, Solomon.

Now Adonijah, whose mother was Haggith, put himself forward and said, "I will be king." So he got chariots and horses ready, with fifty men to run ahead of him. (His father had never rebuked him by asking, "Why do you behave as you do?") (1 Kings 1:5-6)

David never rebuked him. He never interfered. Some translations say, *"David never crossed him."* It literally means he *never caused him pain.* It also means he *never fashioned or formed him into shape.* But isn't this what parents are supposed to do? They fashion and form children into shape. This happens when a mother or father pulls out the parental sandpaper to sand down behavior and attitudes that are out of line. Parents sand this behavior because they love their children, care for them, and want them to succeed in the future. Good parents are not irresponsible with their responsibility.

All children are precious when they enter the world. They look so cute and innocent. But every baby is born a sinner with a selfish bent. If left to ourselves, each of us will behave however we are allowed to behave. Left to ourselves, we all will naturally desire to do whatever we want to do, when we want to do it. If allowed, it will eventually lead to disastrous results. Some children seem to naturally have tender hearts. Others are naturally bent for rebellion. Some children respond to correction and discipline quickly, while others seem to only respond when they experience the consequences of hitting the hard pavement of life.

When I was disciplined as a child, I remember my parents saying, *"This is going to hurt me more than it's going to hurt you."* What? They weren't the one feeling the sting of their bottom getting spanked, or the pain of staying home on Friday nights instead of hanging out with friends. This made no sense to me

LEFT TO OURSELVES, WE ALL WILL NATURALLY DESIRE TO DO WHATEVER WE WANT TO DO, WHEN WE WANT TO DO IT.

until I became a parent. Disciplining a child you love is no fun. It is tiring, emotionally draining, and a real inconvenience to enforce penalties. It is not easy at all. But doing what is easy is rarely profitable.

I wrote a book on parenting called *Dream House: Blueprints to a Healthy and Happy Home*. Each chapter represented a different room in a home, with principles to parent your child and teenager. The room I symbolically used to represent discipline was the laundry room. What would your home be like without the ability to do laundry? What parent would allow their child or teenager to consistently go out in public with clothes that have nasty stains on them or smell to high heaven? It would be embarrassing to a child, especially a teenager, and to the parent as well if this happened. But this is exactly what happens when a parent enables their child. Everyone sees the stain or smells the odor of unattended actions or attitudes that have been ignored.

When King David enabled his children, he sent them out into the world with stains and odors that everyone could see and smell. David did not have the courage or fortitude to tell his kids, *"No, you're not going to do that. You will not be allowed to act this way!"* David never required them to face consequences. David was an enabler. When we enable, our irresponsibility will end up being someone else's responsibility.

Why Do People Enable?

Why does enabling still continue when most people are aware that it is bad? Many people enable because they allow their emotions to trump their responsibility. Because they feel so much love and mercy for their child, friend, or spouse, they find it too difficult to confront them. Other people enable because they hope or assume someone else will do the hard work of confrontation. They justify in their mind, *"I'll just love them, and surely someone else will confront them."*

Enablers know their friend is making poor choices and not meeting their responsibilities, so they worry. They worry their friend will be laid off, get hurt, go bankrupt, go to jail, or possibly even die. These concerns cause them to help and protect their friend from **ENABLING KEEPS THE STATUS QUO, WHICH IS THE EASIEST AND MOST CONVENIENT PATH TO TAKE.** the disastrous consequences they can see coming. They desperately want their friend to stop using drugs, start making wiser choices, stop hanging around bad people, and start growing up. They know from experience they can't make their friend change by nagging, threats, or begging, so they continue to help and protect. Ultimately their need to try to control the situation, combined with a deep emotional fear of what could happen, causes them to enable their friend.

Another reason people continue to enable is choosing short-term relief over long-term health. The truth is, confronting destructive behavior is difficult, and creates a real threat that it might change the current status of their relationship. It is easier to just let things slide. A genuine change in attitude or behavior of the culprit is not quick. Real change is typically a long process with plenty of ups and downs, which is exhausting. Enabling keeps the status quo, which is the easiest and most convenient path to take.

Denial is also a powerful force that causes people to continue carrying the baggage of enabling. Everyone is different when it comes to denial, but it ultimately results in people not facing the truth of their situation. Take the fed-up wife of a husband who drinks too much. She lives quietly in her home, choosing to spend more time with her friends or working with hobbies, while saying nothing to her husband about his drinking problem. Her silence is a form of enabling but she justifies it because she did not do anything to contribute to her husband's addiction. Why does she stay silent? Because she thinks to herself, *"If I say something to him about it and he turns out to be an alcoholic, I would have to make choices that I am not ready to make."* Her mind jumps to divorce or separation, but she knows she is not ready for those either. She is in her sixties and realizes that a divorce or separation would turn her world upside down. She ultimately resigns herself to believing that this is just how it is going to be, and thus creates a whole life with him, absorbing all the fallout of a life with an alcoholic.

Another reason for the continuation of enablement is guilt. For some, the guilt is real. They know they failed to do the hard work years earlier, so they blame themselves more than the culprit. Whether it was because they were absent, lazy, or selfish for failing to confront the problem, they continue to enable because of the blame they put on themselves. For others, the guilt they feel is actually false guilt. They might think, *"What did I do to contribute to this? Surely I could have done more."* Because some people think they are the cause of the problem, they also erroneously believe they can fix it. These are the people who bail their kids or spouse out of jail because they do not want others in the family, neighborhood, or church to find out, which would only make them feel even more at fault. This type of cyclical reasoning is all about keeping the status quo in order to keep the family secrets.

Enabling only accomplishes three things:

1. It gives an enabler a false sense of control. Enabling may temporarily reduce your fear and anxiety, but ultimately your own well-being is compromised.
2. Enabling always prolongs poor behavior and postpones recovery. Every time you fix the situation, they learn that no matter how irresponsibly they act, there are no consequences. Because you will take care of everything, there is always another chance. They never hit bottom.
3. Enabling will leave you frustrated, discouraged, and hopeless. One day you will wake up and realize that all of your effort, all of your great counsel, and all of the time, money, and energy spent is not working. In fact, it has never worked.

What to Do
The action step for the enabler is simple, but difficult to do. You have to STOP. You can't gradually stop. You must immediately stop. The problem you are contributing to will not go away. In fact, it will get worse. It may never end until you stop trying to fix it. The first step in setting down this secret baggage of enabling is to recognize there is a problem and what you are doing is not only not working, it is wrong. You cannot control your loved one, but you can control and change how you respond to them.

God's approach to fixing a problem is to allow painful consequences to surface. Consequences are some of the best teachers that most humans learn from. If there were not pain, we probably would not ever learn. My mother told me something years ago that I have never forgotten. She said, *"Barry, sometimes God has to unfix what we're trying to fix so that He can fix what needs to be fixed."* In my experience, God seems to wait for us to stop so He can start making things right.

Sarah (name changed for privacy) was on my youth staff in California who worked with a special group of thirty troubled teenagers who had run away from home, were addicted to drugs, and had dropped out of school. Some of them were even homeless because their parents had kicked them out of the house. These teenagers had spiked hair, body piercings, wore dark clothes, and covered their heads with hoodies while they lit up their cigarettes around the corner from the main entrance to our high school amphitheater. They had little to no interest in joining the hundreds of high school students who came to our midweek gatherings. They viewed those students as too preppy, too good, and too uncomfortable to be around. Instead of forcing these teenagers to come into our lobby or amphitheater, we provided a special space for them around the side of the building by our large storage units. This ministry to troubled teens made some people— mainly parents—nervous. They referred to it as our "smokers' ministry." Several parents asked if I would disband this group because they did not want "these types of kids" to negatively influence their own

GOD'S APPROACH TO FIXING A PROBLEM IS TO ALLOW PAINFUL CONSEQUENCES TO SURFACE.

kids. I refused. As tough a crowd as they appeared to be, these teenagers were ready to receive the love of God. Each of the leaders had a unique perspective to lead this unique ministry. Each leader had once been where these troubled teenagers were.

One Wednesday night, I came over to say hello to this group as well as encourage the leaders for their good work. Sarah was in her mid-twenties, with a few tattoos and piercings, but with a sparkle of joy in her eyes. I asked her why she had a passion for working with these teenagers. She told me her story.

> I grew up in this church and come from a wonderful Christian family. When I was a teenager, I started hanging around the wrong friends and soon began experimenting with drugs and alcohol. Over time, I slowly withdrew from my church friends, church, and eventually God. My new friends were everything to me so I didn't care.
>
> Slowly, I found myself addicted to drugs, which drove me deeper into the drug culture, and my "friends" kept pushing me deeper down a dark hole. Whenever I hit bottom I would always come home, and my parents would let me stay there while I recovered. There was always plenty of food and a

warm bed. My mom and dad would plead, beg, and reason with me to get help. But each time I would refuse and eventually head back out for some more "fun." Sometimes I didn't return home for weeks at a time. Many nights I wouldn't know where I was sleeping and I would wake up clueless about what had happened the night before.

My drug addiction worsened, so I started stealing to pay for my hits. The same pattern would happen—I would hit bottom, come home, enjoy a warm bed and loving parents and then head back out again. But now I started stealing cash and jewelry from my parents. When confronted by them, I lied right to their faces. I was getting more and more defiant, more verbally abusive towards them, and completely out of control. They cried more, pleaded harder, and I would just spit back in their faces with my attitude, language, and actions. Because I knew no matter what I did, my parents would always welcome me back home. Of course they would. They are my parents.

One day, after angrily yelling at my parents, I slammed the door as I headed out to get back with my "friends" and "fun." This time, I stayed away longer and went deeper than ever before. Eventually I stumbled home, arriving in the early morning hours. I put my key in the front door and it didn't work. I thought I was at the wrong house, so I doubled-checked. My parents' cars were in the driveway. I tried my key again. No luck. I started pounding on the door in anger. How dare they change the locks on me! I'm their daughter, for goodness' sake! After a few minutes, the curtains by the front door slowly pulled back and I saw Mom and Dad peeking out. I yelled at them to open the door. What they said next shocked me. They told me I had to leave, and that I was no longer welcome until I got clean. I exploded. I cussed them out and told them how much I hated them. I was glad when I saw them crying; it served them right. As I stomped away, deep down I knew they loved me. Deep down I knew they were right. And I also knew how deeply I had just hurt them. But in my anger, I stuffed those feelings and stormed off.

Without the comfort of home, I crashed hard. Really hard. My safety net was gone. What my parents did to me did hurt me, but I now consider it the best thing they ever did for me. When they stopped enabling me by always welcoming me home, they forced me to get the help I needed. It took some time but eventually I came home clean, healthy, and free again. It still kills me to think of how much I hurt them. I hurt the sweetest, most loving parents a daughter could ever have. But I am so grateful they did what was so incredibly hard for them to do. I am not sure I would be alive today if they hadn't locked me out that night.

Working with these troubled teenagers is a joy for me. I see myself in so many of them. I am trying to show Jesus to them and let them know that someone understands what they're going through. I am also here to show them that someone loves them no matter how they look, talk, or act. I have been in that dark place. Thankfully, I was able to come back to the other side.

What Are the Signs?
One sign of enablement is when the responsible one is often miserable and the irresponsible one is often happy. This actually makes sense because the one being enabled is getting their way and does not feel the pressure to fix their problem. They have come to believe that it is not really their problem at all. It is human nature to feel good when we can avoid consequences.

Another sign of enablement is ungratefulness from the one being enabled. You would think the opposite would occur, but it rarely does. Enablement grows a sense of entitlement and whatever is given, ignored, or fixed for them is somehow deserved. I say entitlement "grows" because early on there are words of appreciation and comments like, *"This will never happen again. I will pay you back. I promise!"* However, an attitude of ungratefulness eventually blossoms. We are not naturally grateful for what we believe is owed to us.

Enabling also leads to resentment. People who are enabled usually end up resenting the people who try to help them. Again, enabling is often disguised as helping, but it actually hurts them by making them dependent. Dependency leads to frustration, and frustration leads to resentment. I know of people who gave and gave and helped and helped, who were shocked and deeply hurt to find out the loved one they helped has become resentful of them. This is counterintuitive, but sadly true.

To the Enabled
If you are reading this and you are the one with a pattern of being sheltered from facing the consequences of your own attitudes or actions, please read carefully. I write this with love, care, and most importantly, with honesty. The sooner you take responsibility for your life, your actions, and your attitudes, and stop playing the victim, the sooner you will become a responsible person who is admired and respected. That may hurt but it needs to be said. The truth is, people who are enabled are not admired nor respected. People may pretend to respect you but they do not. In fact, they talk to others about how you act, and it is not pretty. Immaturity is never admired or respected. Immaturity is expected of little children, but it loses its charm as one gets older. There is one word that sums up maturity: *responsible*. Being responsible to own our faults, to do what is asked of us, to obey the rules, and to follow through with what we promised are all examples of maturity; these are examples of one who is worthy of being admired and respected.

ENABLING IS NOT LOVE. IT FEELS LIKE IT, BUT IT IS NOT.

If you grow up and become more responsible, you will slowly unpack your "secret" baggage that is not really a secret to everyone around you. It will be difficult. It will be painful. But deep down inside, you will feel better about yourself like never before. And so will others.

To the Enabler
What I am about to write may be hard for you to read. But you have to hear it, because I do not want you to be an Eli, a David, or someone who is irresponsible with your responsibility. Here are four tips so that you can stop carrying around the secret baggage of being an enabler.

My first tip is: *Stop trying to fix what God is trying to fix, by allowing consequences to do their job.* Parents, start when your children are young by not picking up their toys for them. If they are old enough to pull the toys out of the box to play with them, they are old enough to put them back in the box when they are done playing with them. You are teaching them an important lesson in life: if you make a mess, you must clean up the mess. One time when my children were young, for discipline purposes I gathered up all the toys left on the floor, put them in a black garbage bag, and grounded them in the garage for one week. When the toys finally were set free again, the next time I told my children to put their toys away or have them taken away for another week, it was amazing to see every single toy put away. They did not want to face the consequences of having their toys grounded again.

The second tip is: *Allow things to get worse.* If your children are older, stop doing their homework or projects for them. Help them, yes, but stop doing it for them. "But I want them to get a good grade." Great; let them earn the grade themselves. You are not helping them. You are harming them. "But I love them and if I don't do it for them their grades are going to drop, and they'll be ineligible to play sports." Enabling is not love. It feels like it, but it is not. Stop covering for them. Stop fixing the problem for them. "But that's hard." Absolutely! Let things get worse. Allow consequences and accountability to do their jobs, even if things get worse.

The third tip is: *Avoid feeling guilty.* When you stop enabling, you are going to feel guilty. Those who have been enabled have a Ph.D. in manipulation. You need to say, "No, I am not going to do that for you. You have to face it, own it, and be accountable for it." If you enabled them in the past, they are going to do all they can to make you feel guilty in the present. Don't fall for it. Don't pick it up. Do not carry that guilt.

My final tip is this: *Allow the hurt to help.* When people have to face and bear the weight of their choices, and it hurts them, allow it. The hurt will actually help them. When clear boundaries have been violated, allow the full pain of consequences to be felt. Removing consequences after the appearance of remorse or repentance is positioning yourself to be manipulated—again. If they are grounded for a week, let it be a full week. If they have to repay you $300, do not call it good after $250 has been paid. If they are told to move out by the end of the month, make it happen. Even if you have to move their stuff outside and change the locks, do it. Let the consequence fulfill its course. You are not being mean. You are just refusing to enable them anymore. You are also allowing the principle of sowing and reaping, from Galatians 5, to do its job. Maybe, just maybe, they will someday think to themselves, *"Oh, that hurts. I don't think I'll do that again."*

There was a man who was reading the paper as he walked out of his hotel. He turned left, took three steps, did not see a large hole in the sidewalk, and fell into the hole. Bruised and bleeding, he climbed out of the hole and went on his way. The next morning he left the hotel, turned left, took three steps, saw the hole, but still fell into it. Bruised and bleeding again, he climbed out of the hole and went on his way. The third morning the man walked out of his hotel and stopped. He looked to his left and saw the hole. He then walked straight, crossed the street, turned left and walked away without falling into the hole.

Chapter Four

Abandonment

In 2008 I went on a short-term mission trip with my church to the untouchable regions of India. These are the areas where the government refuses to provide financial aid or other help, because these people are deemed unworthy due to their status at the lowest level of their caste system. Our teams went to villages to share the good news about Jesus to people who had never even heard of the name *Jesus*.

Every village we entered had various shrines where people sacrificed their own meager food or money to one of their many gods. Some shrines were at the base of a tree. Others were next to a large rock. Their culture teaches a sacrifice must be made in order to appease their gods. When we told them the Son of God, Jesus, left heaven to die on a cross as the sacrifice for their sins, many were astonished. Most had never heard of this good news. As a result, it was not uncommon to see entire villages choosing to reject the millions of gods they had always worshipped, and placing their faith solely in Jesus as the Savior of their soul. This was the best part of the trip.

The most difficult part of this trip was our visit to a leper colony. Not only had their government rejected them, but even their untouchable villages did the same. When a mother with leprosy from this colony found out I was a father of three girls, she told the translator to wait and she rushed off only to return with her healthy young daughter. As she pushed her little girl towards me she pleaded, *"Take her. Please take her with you so she doesn't get what I have."* As hard as it was to tell her I could not grant her request, this still was not the saddest part of my time in India.

The most heartbreaking part of this trip was visiting an orphanage of children abandoned by their parents because of utter poverty and an inability to provide. The following story told to me was all too common for many of these children. The parents would tell their little boy and girl that they were taking a special trip as a family. They packed up their paltry possessions and made their way to the train station where they would sleep under the stars before the train ride in the morning. Understandably, the kids would be bouncing with excitement and filled with anticipation of this special trip on the train they had only seen from a distance. Their parents would feed them, and everyone would bed down for the night. After the children were finally fast asleep, the parents would quietly slip away in the middle of the night and leave. These poor children would wake up confused, scared, and lonely as their parents were nowhere to be found. These abandoned children were, at best, rescued by an orphanage or, at worst, sold into a life of sexual bondage.

Thankfully, the children at the orphanage we visited were not only being loved and cared for, but many of them had also been rescued into a relationship with Jesus Christ that turned their abandonment into a new life of freedom and joy.

Heavy Weight to Bear
Most likely you have never faced this degree of abandonment before, but it is a real issue that many people have faced, either directly or indirectly, in their lives.

The baggage of abandonment is one of the heaviest pieces of emotional baggage to carry around. While some people are fully aware of the pain that abandonment has brought to their lives, many others are completely unaware of the source of their pain. They know they are carrying hurt, frustration, and unhappiness, but they cannot put a finger on its cause. It is like part of them is dead, paralyzed, or numb.

Merriam-Webster dictionary gives us several definitions of being abandoned.[1] The first one is harsh but real. It means *left without needed protection, care, or support*. This definition expresses a sense of finality, of being deserted or being forsaken. Another definition is not quite as harsh, but just as painful. It means *no longer held or thought of; given up*. This definition conveys a sense of rejection, hopelessness, and despair. Both definitions are true. Both cause a great deal of pain that often cause people to withdraw, put up walls, or react out of desperation.

Faultless Abandonment

There are several causes for abandonment. The first one is faultless abandonment, meaning no one did anything wrong. When someone dies from a sickness, an accident, or even old age, it can leave a sense of abandonment for those who love and dearly miss them. Although no one was at fault, those left behind can suffer from a loss of needed care, protection, and support. The same thing is true when someone close to us moves away. It was not wrong for them to move away, but no matter how much we try to stay in contact with them, their absence still affects us deeply. It is hard because our heart was attached to theirs. This is a faultless abandonment.

Little children can suffer from abandonment issues because they have a difficult time understanding and processing the loss of someone special to them. They are too young to understand why they can't see the person anymore. Thankfully, most children who face loss at a very young age grow up and do not remember the actual memories, or even the pain they once experienced.

Other children, however, can struggle without knowing all the implications of the issue of abandonment. My father died of colon cancer when he was fifty-two and I was twenty-seven. He was a fantastic father. As an adult, I experienced all the levels of grief and although I still greatly miss him to this day, I never felt abandoned by him. My younger siblings, Brendie and Bradley, are different. She was nine and he was six when our family buried our father. Their memories of our father are foggy at best, but still painful to this day.

Bradley is now married with two precious and adorable children. He told me once that he still struggles to watch Monday Night Football because he vaguely remembers my father watching the game while being in so much pain. He associates Monday Night Football with a painful experience. My sister, Brendie, is a wife and mother of three charming but rambunctious little boys. At my oldest daughter's wedding, Brendie quietly slipped away when it was time for my father-daughter dance with Ashley. It was too painful. Even though my brother Bobby and I walked Brendie down the aisle for her wedding and tried our best to fill the void of the absence of our father in her life, she was unable to have her father-daughter dance on her special day. Although Brendie loves her older brothers, we can never fully fill the hole that remains in her heart.

Thankfully, Brendie and Bradley had what many people lack: a family who intentionally tried to help them process a significant loss in their formative years. As a family, we are all so proud of Brendie and Bradley and grateful they are thriving with their own families. But the hole left from my father's passing is still a void in their lives. They each have the inevitable baggage that a faultless abandonment brings when there is a death of a parent.

Free Choice Abandonment
The second type of abandonment is free choice abandonment. Someone made a decision to check out, leave, or walk away. This choice captures both parts of the definition of being abandoned: *left without needed protection, care, or support,* and *no longer held or thought of; given up.*

Suicide is in this category. It is a death, of course, but someone made a choice to die. For whatever reason, what they were facing was too much for them, so they quit. They escaped. They convinced themselves it would be better for them, and for those who loved them, if they were to die. They somehow thought this fateful decision was a selfless act but for the friends and family left behind, it was the most selfish thing anybody could ever do. As a result, people felt deserted and abandoned.

Divorce is another free choice abandonment. Sometimes, in the worst cases, divorce makes sense to the adults involved. But many children and teenagers of divorce often believe that somehow the divorce was their fault. *"If I were a better child, he would have stayed." "It must have been my fault my parents gave up."* In most every situation this rationale is not remotely true, but the feelings of abandonment still remain.

Some adopted kids, depending how old they were when they were adopted and the conditions surrounding the adoption, can struggle with abandonment. If no one is there to lovingly and honestly help them process their situation, these kids can grow up thinking, *"Why didn't my parents want me? There must be something wrong with me!"*

Abandonment can also be experienced when a friendship suddenly dissolves. Something was said or not said, something happened or did not happen, or somebody else lied and the lie was believed without confirmation. You are not sure what happened but now he appears to be avoiding you. Someone you thought was your friend now does not answer her phone or return your phone calls, texts, or emails. This causes you to be concerned, confused, and perplexed. Then, when you finally see this friend they are distant, vague, and awkward in your presence. Whether a friendship ends like this or ends in an avalanche of anger and accusations, you feel abandoned by someone who said they cared about you. Whatever the reason, they chose to abandon you and your relationship.

Reactions to Abandonment

Here is the challenge with abandonment: different people respond differently. Some keep it a secret. They do not share it. Instead, they stuff it. When people ask them how they are doing, they do not say, "I'm feeling abandoned today." If they were that honest, people wouldn't know how to respond. They might give an awkward look and walk away, making things feel worse. That is why it is called secret baggage. As a result, some keep relationships at arm's length, avoid commitment, struggle to trust people, or live a life of emotional numbness.

Other people travel down a path of extreme reactions to abandonment. One extreme is a disproportionate amount of attachment. When this happens, people desperately seek attachment to anyone and everyone who will show them any amount of kindness, love, and attention. If this happens, they latch onto that relationship. It is almost as if they are asking, "Am I okay? Do you like me? Will you keep liking me?" Or without saying it, they are thinking, *"You won't leave too, will you?"* As a result, people around them start backing away, thinking quietly, *"Man, I was just trying to be nice. I was just being friendly."* For someone

FOR SOMEONE WITH ABANDONMENT ISSUES, ATTENTION AND CARE ARE LIKE A LIFELINE. THEY JUST GRAB ONTO IT, RELENTLESSLY.

with abandonment issues, attention and care are like a lifeline. They grab onto it, relentlessly. But they end up pushing people away, making the problem worse.

The other extreme is the attitude, *"I don't need anybody."* Maybe when you were young and tension surfaced in the home, your mother would check out and turn to alcohol for comfort. Pretty soon, alcohol consumed her. Eventually, one day your mother walked out of your family. Then when your dad remarried, your attitude toward his new wife was, *"I want nothing to do you. You're not my mother. You'll never be my mother."* You do this to protect yourself and end up building an emotional wall. You convince yourself she is not getting in, because you do not need her. You convince yourself that you do not need anybody. Then you find yourself married one day, but you allow your spouse to get only so close to you. Because of this, at some point either husband or wife hits a relational or emotional brick wall. Deep inside your mind, you believe, *"One day they may leave me. Fine. I didn't really need them to begin with."* This extreme reaction ends up pushing people away who truly love you. You cannot feel their genuine love, because you are in bondage to your abandonment baggage.

Other symptoms of abandonment include resistance toward others, insecurity, flashes of anger, sleeping disorders, eating disorders, and a continual need for reassurance. Some have a fear of being alone and go through life with a constant fear of the future. There are also those who have difficulty trusting anyone, including God. Your heart was damaged. Your trust was broken. You do not fully live; you exist. It is not going to get better until you do something about it.

Abandonment in the Bible
There are a number of examples of people in the Bible who faced abandonment. I am reminded of Joseph, in the book of Genesis. Joseph did not just irritate his older brothers like the average little brother irritates his siblings. He irritated them so much that they were determined to kill him. However, they had a slight change of heart and an influx of mercy, so they decided to sell him into slavery instead. Joseph was truly abandoned by his brothers.

King David writes in Psalm 55 about going to the Tabernacle with one of his good friends to worship God. But his friend had turned on him, abandoning him. He said, *"If it was an enemy I could withstand that."* As a hardened soldier, being rejected by an enemy or an unfriendly acquaintance would not have hurt David. In fact, he would not have spent much emotional energy on it. But David says, "Instead, it is you —my equal, my companion and close friend. What good fellowship we once enjoyed as we walked together to the house of God" (Psalm 55:13-14 NLT).

Can you feel the pain dripping off the pages of this Psalm? Maybe you can relate because you have lost a friend, or an associate, or maybe a business partner stabbed you in the back. It hurt you deeply, and the pain still lingers.

The closest friends of Jesus abandoned him in his darkest hour on earth. Most of them ran for the hills in fear, but Peter's abandonment of Christ was brutal. After everything Peter saw, heard, and experienced with Jesus you would think Peter would be the last disciple to abandon Christ. But he did. When asked by a woman if he was a disciple of Jesus, Peter said he was not. A short while later someone else asked him the same question. He denied it again. When a little slave girl confronted him, Peter denied even *knowing* Jesus. Jesus even felt abandoned by God, his Father, when he was dying for our sins on the cross. He cried out, *"My God, my God, why have you forsaken me?"* This was the epic abandonment.

EVERYONE COMES WITH BAGGAGE. FIND SOMEONE WHO LOVES YOU ENOUGH TO HELP YOU UNPACK.

Other people in the Bible faced abandonment. Joshua was crushed after Moses had died. Ruth believed God had abandoned her through the death of her husband and sons. The Apostle Paul was deserted by his friend Demas while he was in prison in Rome, and faced his death sentence without anyone by his side.

How did they handle their abandonment? What did they do? What should you do?

There is Help

I once saw a picture posted on Facebook with a caption that said, *"Everyone comes with baggage. Find someone who loves you enough to help you unpack."* Thankfully, you have a Heavenly Father who loves you more than you can comprehend and who is there to help you unpack any abandonment baggage you may have, so that this unresolved baggage will not continue to linger or hurt in your life.

One of my heroes in the Bible is the hero of many. Once again, I am referring to David. He is flawed, raw, and passionate, just like you and me. As a result, he writes in a way that most of us can identify with. Psalm 68 is like many of his psalms. It is a contrasting song that launches with an eruption of emotion, and then finishes with a thoughtful theology of God.

OUR HEAVENLY FATHER WILL BE THE FATHER FOR THOSE WITHOUT ONE. GOD WILL DEFEND THE DEFENSELESS WIDOWS, AND GOD WILL TAKE CARE OF THE LONELY.

He begins by telling God what he thinks God should do to those who have hurt him, left him, or abandoned him.

> May God arise, may his enemies be scattered; may his foes flee before him. May you blow them away like smoke—as wax melts before the fire, may the wicked perish before God. (Psalm 68:1-2)

That's right, God! Blow them away like smoke, and make them melt while you're at it! For those who have caused deep pain and wounds of abandonment, this sounds just about right to me. Then David begins to calm down.

> But may the righteous be glad and rejoice before God; may they be happy and joyful. Sing to God, sing in praise of his name, extol him who rides on the clouds; rejoice before him —his name is the Lord. (Psalm 68:3-4)

How is this possible, David? It is hard to worship God when we are filled with the agony of abandonment. David understands this because he has practiced what he is now preaching to us. What he writes next is vitally important. He begins to describe who God is and why we should worship Him in our pain. "A father to the fatherless, a defender of widows, is God in his holy dwelling. God sets the lonely in families, he leads out the prisoners with singing" (Psalm 68:5-6).

David describes a list of those who have been abandoned: the fatherless, the widows, the lonely, and those in bondage. Further, David describes what God does to help them. Our Heavenly Father will be the father for those without one. God will defend the defenseless widows, and God will take care of the lonely. The phrase "God sets the lonely in families" literally means, *He settles the lonely at heart*. How beautiful. How calming. But the best part is the last part: God will set the prisoners free from the bondage of abandonment.

If you have ever experienced abandonment, it feels like you are in a prison. You are confined, trapped by your circumstances. You can't move forward in life. You are trapped by a decision someone else has made. But with God, *"he leads forth the prisoners with singing."* Being set free will cause us to rejoice, celebrate, sing, maybe with a happy dance thrown in. That is what freedom from bondage looks like.

If you are going to move forward in life, you will have to lean in to God. And God, over time, will restore you, healing you from the inside out. Is it a quick fix? Absolutely not! Is it hard? Most definitely!

I like how the Apostle Paul faced his abandonment issues. Paul was in prison, facing numerous court trials. The outcome did not look promising. Paul then communicated to some friends, asking them to come and be with him at these trials. He needed their support and encouragement; just their presence would mean so much to him. Here is what happened and how Paul responded.

"At my first defense, no one came to my support, but everyone deserted me. May it not be held against them" (2 Timothy 4:16). No one showed up. He felt let down. He felt abandoned, because he *was* abandoned. But then Paul made a critical choice—he was not going to hold it against them. That is a difficult but powerful first step. Holding it against those who abandoned him was not going to help Paul one bit. Holding it against them was only going to hurt Paul all the more. Then Paul gives the reason behind his decision to move forward without holding a grudge.

> But the Lord stood at my side and gave me strength...The Lord will rescue me from every evil attack and will bring me safely

to his heavenly kingdom. To him be glory for ever and ever. Amen. (2 Timothy 4:17-18)

If we are going to find healing in this area of abandonment we are going to have to lean on God, and fully trust in Him. When we begin to trust in God He will, over time, allow our trust in other people to be restored through Him. Maybe one day you can look back and say, "The Lord was at my side, and He gave me strength." Here are four reasons why you can start placing your trust in God to help you experience freedom from your abandonment baggage.

God is Patient

We can trust in God because God is patient with us. How many times do we withdraw from God? How many times do we quit on God? How many times do we hurt Him? We abandon God, but He says His mercies toward us are new every morning. God does not give us what we deserve. Not only are His mercies new every morning, but His grace is sufficient for us. His love is unfailing. And His love endures forever. God gives His patience to us. Wow!

What can we do with someone who is struggling with abandonment issues? Abandonment does not just disappear. It is a slow-healing wound. Be patient with them. Be patient with a child who has gone through this. Be patient with a spouse. Be patient with a friend who struggles with this. Be patient with yourself. Because God is patient with you, you are able to be patient with others.

God is Honest

The second reason we can trust God is that He is honest with us. Trust is the foundation of every relationship. When we can't trust someone, it is hard to tell if they are lying to us or being truthful. However, God is truth. It is the nature of God to always speak truth. There is truth in Scripture that is enjoyable to hear, and there is truth in Scripture that is difficult to hear. But God tells us His truth because He loves us.

TAKE THE TIME TO LOOK IN THE MIRROR AND FACE YOUR ABANDONMENT ISSUES AND NEEDS.

Likewise, we need to be honest. The first person you need to be honest with is yourself. Take the time to look in the mirror and face your abandonment issues and needs. Be honest enough to admit you are struggling. Admit you are hurting. Admit you have unresolved abandonment issues. Be honest enough to seek out a professional counselor if you need help digging out from under your past hurts. Keep going until you become healthy in this area.

We also need to be honest with the people close to us, especially the people who love us. Letting them in on your abandonment pain may help them understand you like never before. You will be allowing them to pray for you, encourage you, and love you more deeply than ever before. But do not be shocked if they are not surprised. They may not know all the details of your pain, but many times our secret baggage is not a secret to people around us. Yes, it is a risk to open up with those you love and trust. But it is a healthy risk that is incredibly worth taking.

If you are a parent or grandparent and have a child who has gone through some type of abandonment, be honest with them. Talk with them gently and allow them to begin processing any pain they may have. If you have an adopted child and you have yet to tell them the truth of their adoption story, be honest with them and tell them, the earlier the better. Be tactful, discerning, and ask God for wisdom, but be honest with them. Please do not allow any fear you may have that they would rather be with their biological parents stop you from loving them enough to be honest with them. In every case of adoption that I have personal experience with, the adopted child has always wanted to have some type of connection with their biological parents. In the end, they have always viewed their adopted parents as their real parents because of the love, care, and comfort they received from them. However, every time the adopted parent kept the adoption story a secret, it has always come back to bite them in a painful way. Honesty is always the best policy.

God Assures Us
The third reason why we can trust God is His assurance that He is always with us. Joshua, who had followed Moses since he was young, found himself paralyzed without his mentor. Moses was dead and Joshua was in charge of several million strong-headed and complaining Israelites. I love how God tenderly assured Joshua over and over of His presence.

As I was with Moses, so I will be with you; I will never leave you nor forsake you. Be strong and courageous, because you will lead these people to inherit the land I swore to their ancestors to give them. (Joshua 1:5-6)

Then a little while later God said, "Have I not commanded you? Be strong and courageous. Do not be afraid; do not be discouraged, for the Lord God will be with you wherever you go" (Joshua 1:9).

Assurance is never realized immediately. We are only assured after being told over and over again. Over time, we start believing it. God reminded Joshua several times that He would be with him. He would not be forsaken. When God says He will never leave you or forsake you, He is saying that He will continually be there for you in heart, mind, and spirit. As long as you are open, He will constantly pour out His heart, His grace, His love, His joy, His wisdom, His peace, and His freedom to you, all for your sake.

God has said, "Never will I leave you; never will I forsake you." So we say with confidence, "The Lord is my helper; I will not be afraid. What can mere mortals do to me?" (Hebrews 13:5b-6)

Here is what the famous preacher, Charles Spurgeon, said about this passage in Hebrews:

I have no doubt you are aware that our translation does not convey the whole force of the original, and that it would hardly be possible in English to give the full weight of the Greek. We might render it, "He hath said, I will never, never leave thee; I will never, never, never forsake thee;" for, though that would be not a literal, but rather a free rendering, yet, as there are five negatives in the Greek, we do not know how to give their force in any other way. Two negatives nullify each other in our language; but here, in the Greek, they intensify the meaning following one after another.[2]

Are you getting the hint? God's assurance is also found in Isaiah 41:10, Deuteronomy 31:6, Zephaniah 3:17, Matthew 28:20, and Romans 8:38-39. God is constantly giving us assurance that we are loved, and He is with us. Others may abandon us, but God never will.

Others may forsake us, but God will not. He stays. He remains. He endures. God will never abandon us.

One way you can help those you love who have abandonment struggles is to shower them with assurance. Remind them that you love them, you accept them, you would marry them all over again. When they act out with their abandonment pain you can say, "No matter how hard you try, or how mean you can be to me, I am not going anywhere because I love you." Assure them. Assure them. Assure them, just like God assures us.

Bre, a wonderful wife and mother of two young children from my church, recently shared her story with me:

> My father was taken away from me on a cold November day in 2013, while I was just thirteen years old. The cause was a house fire. Not just a house fire, but one the fire marshal declared an arson case due to multiple hot spots that started the house fire.
>
> My daddy was the most amazing father. My twin sister and I were his world. He overcame a lot, including alcoholism, to be the amazing father and role model we both needed. He worked his tail off to provide for us. We were so close. Some of my favorite memories were watching *The Lion King* with him every Sunday, belting out our classic tunes with every car ride, and him singing, "You Are My Sunshine" to us. We'd always watch storms together too. He'd bring his recliner onto the front porch, sitting with each of us twins on one leg of his lap. He'd hold us tight and we'd watch the storms roll by. Although it was a scary storm, there was something calming about being in my daddy's arms. He was my protector and I felt as if I could never be harmed. I don't remember going one day without telling each other how much we loved one another.

OTHERS MAY FORSAKE US, BUT GOD WILL NOT. HE STAYS. HE REMAINS. HE ENDURES. GOD WILL NEVER ABANDON US.

In short, we had an amazing relationship that I will forever be grateful for. However, now as a twenty-eight-year-old adult, I'm left scarred by the fact that my time with my father ended so abruptly while I was so young. I still need him. And it pains me that he didn't get to walk me down the aisle or have chance to meet my children, his grandbabies.

My abandonment both did and still does affect me. Right after his death I moved back with my mother—whom I love with all my heart and have an amazing relationship with today. However, she too was overcoming the nasty disease of alcoholism. My twin sister and I had to grow up and mature a bit faster than most. It's like we had to place our childhood in a slingshot, pull it back, and let it go. The truth is we had to practically take care of ourselves growing up while living intermittently with different loving relatives in the surrounding area. Throughout the years, I have always felt that pit of emptiness that I refer to as my "Daddy's Pit." I've missed him so much and felt that he, my children, and I have missed out on so many memories and experiences that most take for granted with their fathers. I have had dreams about how he died which causes anxious questions in my mind such as: *"Did he know what was happening? Did he suffer? Did he try to escape? Most importantly, was he saved? Where is he now?"* These are the thoughts that keep me awake at night from time to time, though I genuinely try to pray through them.

Although I grew up in a family of believers and have always believed, about two years ago I decided to become a follower of Christ, which I whole-heartedly think is different from just believing. I know this "baggage" I deal with has not gotten easier in the sense of missing my dad or fully filling his void, but I do believe it has helped influence many life lessons throughout my life such as: loving my children unconditionally, letting them know I love them (as my daddy did, since I know how much that meant to me), appreciating the father my husband has become, relaying to my children my faith and trust in Christ (what I lacked and wish I knew with my dad), forgiving others since none of us know what will happen the next minute from now, and to just love everyone knowing that they may be suffering though they don't show it and to be that peek of sunshine amidst their storm.

The hardest part in gaining lasting freedom from my abandonment baggage is the person of interest is still walking free today, with not quite enough evidence to bring her to justice. Though we are pretty sure who committed the arson, I am still working on my forgiveness toward her. Reading through the New Testament reminds of how much I have been forgiven by Christ. To be honest, I am still on my healing journey.

Like Bre, you can move forward from the pain of abandonment. It will take time. It may take a counselor. It will most definitely take God's help. Slowly but surely, it is possible to remove this baggage from your life and current relationships, and eventually view it through the rear-view mirror. Hopefully, if and when you recognize someone dragging around this piece of luggage, you can come alongside of him or her and tenderly point them in the direction that eventually leads to freedom.

Chapter Five

Starvation

Abraham Maslow was born in 1908 and raised in Brooklyn, New York. His parents were first-generation Jewish immigrants from Kiev, who escaped the Czarist persecution prior to his birth. His family upbringing was simple and poor, while living in a working-class neighborhood filled with anti-Semitic gangs. On multiple occasions, these gangs chased and threw rocks at Abraham on his walk home. The turmoil outside his home was also felt within it, primarily involving Abraham's relationship with his mother.

As he grew up, Abraham began to loathe his mother's stinginess, her prejudice towards blacks, her exploitation of everyone, her assumptions that she was never wrong, and her lack of love for anyone else in the world—including her own husband and seven children. This caused Abraham to find an escape in libraries and books. It was here that Abraham developed a love for reading and learning. He would eventually earn a master's degree in psychology, teach at universities, and later became famous for what is called *Maslow's Hierarchy of Needs*.[3]

Simply put, Maslow taught that every human has basic needs that must be met in order to develop in life in a healthy way. He broke down our four basic human needs: biological and physiological needs, safety needs, love and belonging needs, and esteem needs. When certain needs are not met, we are stunted in our development. Deficiency needs surface due to deprivation, which motivate people to go on a desperate search for these unmet needs. Also, the motivation to fulfill such needs will become stronger the longer they are denied. For example, the longer a person goes without food, the hungrier they will become. Sadly, the root of Maslow's fame grew from what he had experienced (or did not experience) from his own unhealthy upbringing.

Our next secret baggage is called starvation. This is not about a lack of food or physical malnourishment. This is about being deprived of unconditional love and emotional nourishment. Abraham Maslow described this as being deprived of the need of love and belongingness in the areas of friendship, intimacy, trust, acceptance, and the giving and receiving of affection and love.

Starvation is the emotional side of abandonment. The previous chapter discussed abandonment, which is when someone physically walked away or left you for some reason. However, when your parents were physically present in your life but love was doled out inconsistently, infrequently, and in carefully measured doses, you began to acquire the baggage of starvation.

Performance-Based Love

When love is not given freely or unconditionally, we can become starved from lacking genuine love, acceptance, worth, and security. If by chance love is felt, it most likely comes with conditions. This kind of love is typically attached to a performance from you: if you made high grades, if you made the team, if you played well, if you were chosen for the main role, if you sang well, if you made them look good, and so on. People who experience this type of performance-based love end up feeling a subconscious pressure to continually perform well, so that they will receive something that God designed them to receive from their parents: *unconditional love.*

In the early 1990s, Andre Agassi was the most famous tennis player in the world. Not only was he winning on the tennis court, he was also winning on the television commercial circuit. In 1991, Agassi appeared in his most famous commercial for a camera called the Canon Rebel. In the commercial the good-looking, tanned, cocky, and fashionably attired super-athlete steps out of a white Lamborghini, gazes at the camera, pulls his Ray-Ban sunglasses halfway down his nose and declares, "Image is everything." This statement was more than a line that became popular. It was a statement accurately reflecting who he was more than most people

WHEN LOVE IS NOT GIVEN FREELY OR UNCONDITIONALLY, WE CAN BECOME STARVED FROM LACKING GENUINE LOVE, ACCEPTANCE, WORTH, AND SECURITY.

realized. While he displayed the image of a successful and fulfilled tennis champion, the truth was shockingly the opposite.

In his memoir, *Open*, Agassi describes growing up with a father whose love for him was directly tied to how well he performed on the tennis court. Andre shocked the world when he openly confessed in his book that he hated the game of tennis from the first time he picked up a tennis racket to the day he retired. What drove Agassi to become a champion was not a love and passion for the sport, but his desire to win the heart of his father to love him. He described a father who was unable to "tell the difference between loving me and loving tennis."[4]

Power of Physical Touch
In addition to unconditional love, we all need *emotional nourishment*. This includes verbal affirmation, encouragement, and appropriate physical touch. Affirming, encouraging, and touching are other ways people express love. Saying "I love you" and showing "I love you" is a powerful combination that produces health deep down into the human soul. When unconditional love is connected with emotional nourishment, it produces emotionally healthy children and teenagers who enter adulthood fully equipped to survive a cruel and difficult world. However, if people have been deprived of any of these critical expressions of love, they will be starved of vital ingredients for a successful and healthy life.

I strongly believe that God hard-wired the human body to respond positively to healthy and appropriate physical touch. Researchers have documented the human need for touch. Maia Szalavitz wrote an article about the negative effect caused by the lack of touching.

> Babies who are not held and nuzzled and hugged enough will literally stop growing and if the situation lasts long enough, even if they are receiving proper nutrition, they can die. Researchers discovered this when trying to figure out why some orphanages had infant mortality rates around 30-40%. We now know that orphanages are no place for infants— babies aged zero to five. They simply do not receive enough stimulation in group residential care to develop to the fullest of their capacities.[5]

Beyond infancy, human beings respond to human touch. Consider the following examples shared by Michelle Trudeau in her article, "Human Connections Start with a Friendly Touch."

> If a teacher touches a student on the back or arm, that student is more likely to participate in class. The more athletes high-five or hug their teammates, the better their game. A touch can make patients like their doctors more. If you touch a bus driver, he's more likely to let you on for free. If a waitress touches the arm or shoulder of a customer, she may get a larger tip.

> Hand-holding or hugging also results in a decrease of the stress hormone cortisol, says Matt Hertenstein, an experimental psychologist at DePauw University in Indiana. "Having this friendly touch, just somebody simply touching our arm and holding it, buffers the physiological consequences of this stressful response," Hertenstein says.

> In addition to calming us down and reducing our stress response, a friendly touch also increases release of the oxytocin, also called the "cuddle hormone" which affects trust behaviors. "Oxytocin is a neuropeptide, which basically promotes feelings of devotion, trust and bonding. It really lays the biological foundation and structure for connecting to other people," Hertenstein says.[6]

I have told countless married couples that every spouse should both *know* and *feel* that they are loved. This is also true of children and teenagers. As the old adage says, "Don't just tell me. Show me." Telling is important; showing is just as important. When someone grows up without feeling loved, they will be starved of what they need to both survive and thrive in life.

GOD HARD-WIRED THE HUMAN BODY TO RESPOND POSITIVELY TO HEALTHY AND APPROPRIATE PHYSICAL TOUCH.

There is a special young lady in my church by the name of Victoria (name changed for privacy). She is close with our family and I was honored when she recently shared her story with me.

My father is literally my hero and I love him to death. He was and is present in my life, but it pains me to say that he has not been and is not emotionally present at all. As a result, I found myself craving appropriate physical affection from other people. It later dawned on me that I was craving that affection from my father.

When I saw other girls receiving love and affection from their fathers, it made me long for that myself. It also made me jealous and bitter. Eventually, without this kind of love from my father, it caused me to seek for it in wrong ways. As a result, I grew up not knowing my worth because I was never shown how love was supposed to look. This caused me to have broken relationships and my teenage years were filled with giving myself away in a desperate search for love. It was like living in a prison cell even though the prison door was wide open.

Thankfully, I began to find my worth in Jesus Christ. I have also learned that I deserve to be treated with love, respect, and dignity, and that I do not have to search for these things in all of the wrong places. This has allowed me to start walking in freedom. I am now sharing this same freedom with other young girls who are struggling with their self-worth like I used to.

Even to this day, it saddens me that I did not have a father who was emotionally present when I needed it most. I love my father, but I still search for that love. Of course, it's a process, but every day I am walking towards freedom from the bondage and baggage of experiencing the starvation of love I was born to crave.

One of my healthy distractions from the pressures of being a pastor is volunteering to coach basketball for high school girls in our local community. I first started coaching my own two daughters' teams when they were in junior high, but I continued coaching for years after they both graduated from high school. I coached because, first, I love the game of basketball, and second, it is an incredible opportunity to pour love and encouragement into the lives of teenagers. Sadly, too many players I have coached have been starved for love and encouragement in word, deed, and with appropriate physical touch. It is amazing how powerful a pat on the back, a gentle squeeze on the elbow, an arm around the shoulders, or a tender pat on the top of the head can do. Yes, I have helped plenty of girls improve their outside jump shot. But more importantly to me, a great many players have communicated how much they know that "Coach B" loves them.

When you read about the miracles of Jesus in the New Testament, it is incredible how often Jesus touched people that many people avoided touching. Jesus reached out His hand and touched the eyes of the blind, the skin of the person with leprosy, and the legs of the crippled. Have you ever wondered why Jesus so frequently touched the people He healed, many of whom must have been unattractive, obviously diseased, unsanitary, and smelly? Think about this: with His supernatural divine power He could have easily waved His hand and healed them. Sometimes He healed someone with just the spoken word. At other times, Jesus chose to touch people in the process of healing them. You see, Jesus' mission was not chiefly a healing crusade against disease, but rather a ministry to individual people, many of whom happened to have a nasty disease. He wanted people not only to know of His love but also to feel His love and warmth. So, He touched them. There is power in physical touch.

When Bitter Tastes Sweet
Some choices people make are confusing to me. Have you ever scratched your head in bewilderment when you see someone incredibly sharp, who seemingly has it all together, only to find out that they choose to date or marry someone who is rude, disrespectful, or even abusive to them? It makes no sense; they should date or marry someone who is bright, respectful, and loving like they are. On the surface, it makes zero sense for them to choose someone so far beneath them. Below the surface, however, there is a kind of sense to their choice. The following Scripture begins to explain why this happens. "An open rebuke is better than hidden love!" (Proverbs 27:5).

Rebuke can be a helpful form of verbal correction. Done correctly, rebuking is born out of necessity and based on genuine love. It means, *"I care enough to bring this to your attention because you are out of bounds. You are doing something wrong. You are doing something harmful. I am saying this because I care about you; because I love you."* But verse five takes it to another level. This is not a one-on-one conversation done in private. This is about being rebuked in front of other people. The word "open" in this verse literally means to be *exposed in front of people; to be laid bare.* The word picture in the Hebrew is a like a prisoner of war being carried off into exile. They would be naked, stripped of all their dignity, walking away in defeat. I don't know about you but if I was openly rebuked in front of a crowd I would be thinking, *"This is devastating and embarrassing. This is so incredibly humiliating to be exposed of what I have done wrong in front of a group of people."*

This is exactly what Solomon is getting at. He is saying it would be better to be publicly embarrassed for what you are doing wrong than for someone to love you with a hidden love. This is a type of love that literally means *closed up, withdrawn love.* Oh, there is love in there, but it is silent. It is repressed. It is only doled it out in measured doses. This type of love is not in the open for all to see. It is hidden.

Two verses later we are given the sad reason why many people make incredibly poor choices that completely confuse us. "One who is full loathes honey from the comb, but to the hungry even what is bitter tastes sweet" (Proverbs 27:7).

When I am finished eating a fine-tasting, satisfying meal at a restaurant, I am full. As much as I love desserts, when they bring out the tray of dessert samples that has a slice of cheesecake with strawberry sauce dripping off its side, a slice of double chocolate cake with chocolate filling in the middle, and a slice of blackberry pie with a scoop of vanilla ice cream on top, I find myself thinking, *"No, I'm fine. I don't want any."* For this dessert lover, it makes no sense. At times, being presented with dessert is actually a little repulsive to me because my stomach is letting me know, *"There's no more vacancy in here. I'm not interested, no matter how good it might taste!"*

For many years, my wife and I have had a lunch date at her favorite Mexican restaurant on Fridays. After we are finished eating, she often asks me a question that, after thirty-plus years of marriage, gets the same identical response from me. She asks, "What do you want for dinner?" To which I reply, "I don't know. I'm full." You'd think I would answer with my favorite meal, but I don't. I'm full; I am satisfied.

In the Old Testament, honey was a luxury item. It was something special and out of the ordinary; their special dessert. In this proverb it says the one who is full *loathes honey*. But it is completely different for the hungry. The Hebrew meaning for hungry means *famished*. It is not talking about teenagers with their fast-moving metabolism which leaves them craving food two hours after eating. It is talking about someone who has not had a meal in a long time. This is someone who is malnourished and in some stage of starvation. To these individuals, *even what is bitter will taste sweet*. Specifically, those who are starved for unconditional love and emotional nourishment, even what is bitter, even what is nasty, and even what is unhealthy will taste good. It will taste like dessert to them because they are starving for anything that seems like love, attention, and genuine care to them.

THOSE WHO ARE STARVED FOR UNCONDITIONAL LOVE AND EMOTIONAL NOURISHMENT, EVEN WHAT IS BITTER, EVEN WHAT IS NASTY, AND EVEN WHAT IS UNHEALTHY WILL TASTE GOOD.

It is all too easy to shake our heads in frustration at someone who chooses to be in an unhealthy relationship, and write them off as being insecure or immature by how they act in relationships. Instead, we need to try seeing them through the eyes of genuine compassion. Their unwise choices, insecurity, or immaturity could be another way of them crying out, *"I need help. I need love. I just need someone to love me."*

Crystal grew up having a hard time understand self-worth and love, and how to accept it or receive it for herself. Here is the first part of her story:

> I came from a household where I didn't receive hugs, kisses, or hear "I love you" from my parents or siblings. My parents' dysfunction was taught to us through their actions and how they treated each other. I ached for love and attention. So, growing up, I looked for it anywhere and everywhere I could get it. I watched my friends and their families and how they embraced their parents and vice versa, and I always wished to have that. It never made sense at the time why I never wanted

to be home and always wanted to be somewhere else—where someone else could love me.

Now I understand that I was crying out because I was starving. My parents subconsciously trained me to fear and have no hope in humanity. The hurt they felt is the hurt I would feel. The hopelessness they felt would be how I viewed the world. I always felt stupid as a child. They never took the time to teach me any different. How could they? They were caught up in their own pain they brought on each other. I understand that now.

Two years ago, for the first time in my life, I began to taste some freedom from this baggage called starvation. You see, it was two years ago that I accepted Jesus Christ into my life. Afterward, I really started studying the Word of God. Every. Single. Word. As a result, I found my purpose as a mother and wife through God's Word.

There is one day I will never forget. What may seem simple to most people was monumental to me. It was the day I looked up the word "happy" in the dictionary. As I read its definition, tears began flow from my eyes when I realized that I was finally happy. What God was teaching me, and how he was changing me caused me to soak up this brand-new reality into my life. To read this definition and feel exactly how it was defined was eye-opening, and something completely new to me. Now, my Heavenly Father was bringing me up the way I "should" have been brought up when I was young.

I mentioned earlier that this book is the result of a series I taught in my church a number of years ago. It was a teaching series that triggered more emotional and email responses than I have ever experienced as a communicator. The week I taught on the baggage of starvation, my friend Dave sent me an early-morning email about how the message impacted him.

Bulls-eye! The sermon today was dead center. It hit right on the stuff that I have learned, and have been dealing with over the course of the past couple of years. The things you said about needing to work extra hard at work, and working extra hard to please in order to get back acceptance because of the void, is deadly accurate. I didn't receive a mother's love or a father's love. I was abused. I was neglected. Then I was abandoned and sent to an orphan home, then foster homes. Later I was sent to relatives who abused me some more.

I raised myself and left home when I was sixteen. Adults let me down. I didn't trust anyone. And I had a big wall up. NOBODY was going to hurt me again. For years I would pray to God, asking Him, "What's wrong with me? Why was I so liked by my bosses at work for being number one in everything I did, yet I didn't have a single friend?" It was because no one wanted to be around me. My wife was the only person in my life who loved me unconditionally, except God, of course. But God has rescued me from all this now. Every day I live I thank God for His love and for what He gave me. Every day that I live I think about how I have been changed by this experience.

The ABCs of Moving Forward

Moving forward to health and freedom from the baggage of starvation is not one giant leap. It is moving forward one step at a time. The most important step is always the first step. Without it, you will not gain health and freedom but will remain in bondage. Here are three ABC steps for those who have been starved for love and affection:

A: Actually believe God loves you. I strategically use the phrase *actually believe* because, if you grew up going to church, you probably know in your head that God loves you. More than simply knowing, you need a deep-down-in-your-soul belief that impacts your emotions, decisions, and relationships because you actually believe that God loves you for who you are.

The Bible is filled with passages that describe God's love for you and me. The book of 1 John has one of my favorite passages describing how we can *actually* know the love of God.

This is how God showed his love among us: He sent his one and only Son into the world that we might live through him. This is love: not that we loved God, but that he loved us and sent his Son as an atoning sacrifice for our sins. (1 John 4:9-10)

We do not often use the phrase *atoning sacrifice* in our culture these days. We definitely do not use the theological word that older Bible translations use for this phrase: *propitiation*. But there is a powerful picture in its definition. It means that Jesus paid our sin debt for us. We owed it. Jesus paid for it. The payment came at a very high price: His death on the cross. How much does God love you? Picture Jesus hanging on the cross with His arms spread wide apart and Him saying, "I love you this much!"

Jesus did not come here because we asked Him to, or because we believed in Him and He said, "Oh they love me so much. Because they love me I am going to show them love." No, the opposite is true. Jesus came to earth when we were enemies of God, when we were separated from God. Love brought Jesus to earth and then to the cross. God loved us *first*. Do you actually believe that God truly loves you?

Gary Smalley is a well-known Christian author and conference speaker. One of his most personal and intimate books is called *Change Your Heart, Change Your Life,* where he transparently reveals some of the deep baggage that he kept hidden for most of his life. Gary details how a traumatic situation at the age of eight scarred his life and forced him to go underground with his feelings and fears. His family did not know what happened. Later, his wife never knew. His friends, and the organization he founded, never knew. However, everyone around Gary felt the negative effects from his past. Although the contents inside the baggage were a secret, his baggage caused problems with everyone around him. His marriage had problems because of it. It negatively touched his friendships and those who worked for Gary. Each day people were thinking, *"Oh no, Gary's coming. Is he a good Gary today or a bad Gary?"* All of this happened because of the secret baggage he had carried around for decades.

In this book, Gary shared how he *knew* intellectually that God loved him. But he did not *actually believe* that God loved him, because of all the secret shame, pain, and mistakes he was carrying inside. Knowing and believing are not the same.

Gary shared how his life changed when he actually started believing what he had known for decades: God loves Gary for Gary, including all the good, the bad, and the ugly. When this happened, his heart softened and changed. Once he believed that God truly loved him, his anger dissipated, his marriage began to recover, and people at his corporation said to him, "Gary, you're different. You're actually nice to be around." All this happened because he *actually believed* that God loved him.[7]

B: Break the cycle of starvation. Just because you were starved for unconditional love and affection does not mean your spouse, kids, or grandkids need to be starved like you were. This may be a difficult step to take because you might feel like you are flying blind, but it is an important step toward lasting healing and freedom. John continues in verse 11:

> Dear friends, since God so loved us, we ought to love one another. No one has ever seen God; but if we love one another, God lives in us and his love is made complete in us. (1 John 4:11-12)

Too many people race by this passage without understanding how incredibly powerful and transformational it is. Let's break it down:

- Because God loves us, it should affect our relationships with others.
- Because God loves us, we should be compelled to love others.
- Once we start loving others, God shows Himself. He is revealed in and through us, because we are giving love to other hurting people.
- As a result, God's love begins giving us what is lacking within us. Did you catch that? We begin to receive from God the love we were once starved for. His love is being made complete in us when we love others.

Earlier in this chapter I shared the first part of Crystal's story. She was a girl who grew up starved of the love and affection she desperately needed from her parents. Her life changed the day she trusted in Jesus, and over time grew to truly believe that God loved her. But God was not done. He wanted to give her what was lacking for so many years. Watch how 1 John 4:11-12 comes to life when Crystal begins loving the parents who starved her of love. Notice how the cycle of starvation was broken as a result.

My freedom started to flourish when I began to flee from this all-too-familiar baggage in my life. As a mother I was starting to pass along this generational starvation baggage to my children. With the help of God I experienced it being turned around, one uncomfortable step at a time. I came to realize that I couldn't hold a grudge against my parents. God showed me that they could not and were not capable of giving unconditional love because they didn't know any better. All my parents knew was their own pain and hurt and struggle. They didn't realize what they were doing to their children. So how could I hold something like this against them any longer?

Frankly, I did hold it against them for the first twenty-nine years of my life, until I met God. But now God revealed to me why I must let it go—I was starting to bring that negativity into my children's life. It was time to change. I truly took every word God was teaching me and began to apply it to my life. As a result, I couldn't blame my parents for their lack of guidance, but I could be grateful that God's Word was left behind to help me and allow God to "re-raise" me.

I understand this will take time, and my parents and I have a lot of time to make up. But every day gets better and I love them more than ever before. My parents are being blessed by the changes they have seen in my life and how I have forgiven them and see them for who they really are—God's children, who need help too. Now, we're closer than we ever have been. I am so grateful for this. I can't think where I would be without God saving me and changing my life. Think about it: I'm now being raised by the best Teacher ever!

If you are emotionally starved you will search, like I did, for love in the wrong places. As a result, you will end up passing it on to your children and they will carry this baggage themselves. I apologized to my children for the time lost but explained to them in a way they could understand that God is working on me and they see that. My husband and I have worked so hard these past couple of years to fill our home with the love of God, and it is working. Our children are now excelling in their school and sports activities. They were not doing any of that a couple years ago. My husband's relationship with our son has done a complete one-eighty, and he even coaches other kids completely differently. It's beautiful to watch. We are so blessed. God is so good! If we listen and apply, He works in our lives every time.

C: Confront your God-given needs. This is an advanced step to take when you are stronger, healthier, and beginning to taste your newfound freedom from starvation. This step is a challenge to lovingly confront, if they are still alive, those who starved you of your God-given needs. This may seem scary or impossible. Some of you may think, *"That's crazy. I could never do that."* Read on, and it may give you the courage to try this.

Stu Weber tells an emotionally compelling story in his book, *Tender Warrior*. Stu is a retired pastor now, and he was a highly decorated Vietnam Marine before he became a pastor. But he grew up with a hole in his heart. He never once heard his dad say, "I love you." He never once received any kind of physical affection from him, either. They did not have a hostile relationship, just an empty one. Stu wrote it off as, *"Well, my dad is a World War II generation kind of dad. They just don't do those things."* Years later, as a grown man with teenage sons of his own, Stu realized deep down that he truly wanted to hear those words and feel those feelings of love from his father. He also wanted to change the fact that he had never told his dad he loved him, too.

YOUR HEAVENLY FATHER LOVES YOU SO MUCH THAT HE SENT HIS SON TO DIE FOR YOU. HE EXTENDED HIS ARMS FOR YOU.

One day he finally determined, *"I'm going to tell him I love him. I'll probably be rejected but I'm just going to say it anyway."* The longer he thought about this, another revelation came to him. *"Do you know what? My dad was not trained. I'm going to have to train him."* Stu took a road trip and visited his father. Shortly after arriving, he sat down and told his dad that he loved him. After an awkward silence Stu, still determined, looked his father in the eyes and said, "Dad, I've got to ask you a question. Be honest with me. Do you love me?"

"Of course," his dad replied, "You know I do."

Stu responded back, "Say it. I need to hear it."

His father stumbled over the words and awkwardly said, "I love you."

Stu replied, "Say it again." His father said it again a little stronger, "I love you."

It was a short visit, but well worth the three-hour drive. Before Stu left his father's house another idea crossed his mind. It was another risk he was willing to take. "Give me a hug, Dad. I need a hug." The older Marine returned a blank stare to his younger Marine son.

Stu broke the uncomfortable silence. "Well, then I'm going to hug you." He walked up to his dad and gave him a big hug. It was like hugging a statue. His father's hands hung down, and there wasn't even a pat on the back.

Sometime later Stu took another purposeful trip to see his father again. As soon as he saw him, he said, "Dad, I love you."
"I love you too, son."

"Good," Stu said. At the end of the visit Stu stood up and said, "Dad, I need a hug."

His father's arms lifted a little bit and he returned the hug. The third strategic trip came, and the same ritual continued: words of love shared, followed by a quick hug goodbye. Then the day came that Stu has treasured ever since. It was the day Stu pulled up to his father's house and saw his father coming out of the house with his arms extended. Without prompting, his father gave Stu a huge hug and told him that he loved him.[8]

I don't know how many of you have been starved of unconditional love and affection. But I promise you there are more people with this secret baggage than you realize. If this is your story, I am so sorry. Know this: your Heavenly Father loves you so much that he sent His Son to die for you. He extended His arms for you. And there is coming a day when we will see Christ in Heaven, when I guarantee that He will embrace you as His child.

Emotional starvation can drive someone toward foolish behavior. Some of the foolish behavior in your past is because you were lacking what you desperately needed. I hope today you will start a new beginning by unpacking this secret baggage, so that you will not end up starving the people in your life who need you and your love. It could be the beginning of a new chapter of health and freedom in your life. Allow God to complete in you what has been lacking within you for far too long.

Chapter Six
Father Wound

One Sunday morning I was upstairs in our backstage green room that overlooks the church parking lot. I was praying for the three services that morning, as well as the people who were walking into our church building. I could see them, but they were unaware they were being observed and prayed for. One family caught my eye; it was my friend Tim, his wife, and his youngest teenage son. Tim called out to his wife and, when she turned to look at him, Tim pulled her to his side, causing her to smile. His energetic son saw this and came over to give his mother an expressive, over-the-top hug, causing both mother and son to laugh. Tim followed along with a huge smile on his face.

The reason this warmed my heart was because the Tim I know today is not the man I met years ago. When I first met Tim, he seemed a bit lost as a man, as a husband, and as a father. He was a man who had been worn down by the baggage he carried for far too many years.

This is Tim's story.

> My father was an alcoholic. He was never loving, and very abusive. He never physically hit me, but you don't have to be hit to be abused. He used something far more powerful and impactful: his words. Everything I did was inadequate, and never good enough. And I mean everything. The only way I knew I did a good job at something was if I didn't get yelled at for more than five minutes. As a result, I spent every possible moment away from home to avoid him. It was so bad that my father would even yell at me for not being home to yell at. On the outside, I looked pretty good. I was doing well in school, I played sports, and I had a job; my father required that I hand over to him some of my hard-earned money. I found out later

that my father himself was a victim of child abuse. He was acting out how he had been treated.

Everything came to a head one night when my father started an alcohol-induced fight. It began with him yelling at me and calling me all sorts of bad names. I just wanted to go to bed since I had school the next day. I told my dad, "You're drunk. I am not fighting with you. Good night!" As I proceeded to go to my room, he followed with no intention of letting this end. I shut my bedroom door behind me. I didn't have a lock on my door, so I used the old foot-at-the-base-of-the-door trick. He kept pushing and pushing against me, finally wiggling his head through the opening when I momentarily relaxed pressure on the door. Once his head was inside my room, he too relaxed. Then I slammed the door on his head and closed it. He screamed, "I'll get you to open that door!" He ran to his room and I heard him rummaging for his .357 magnum pistol.

I bolted for the kitchen, fearing he was going to shoot me. I called 911, calmly gave my address, and advised them my dad was going to shoot me. At this point he came into the kitchen and I yelled into the phone, "He's here!" and threw the phone so they could trace the call if needed. My dad came at me swinging. I blocked several punches and then I punched him on the side of his head, knocking him to the ground. At this point, years of fear, frustration, and anger welled up within me as I grabbed a frying pan on the nearby stove. Dumping the contents on the ground, I reared back to hit my father with everything I had. I was literally going to "Hank Aaron" my dad's head with the frying pan, which would have ended his life and my abuse. I stood there for what seemed an eternity but didn't swing. That's when the police came in with me standing over him, frozen, and my dad lying on the ground.

I spent the night at a friend's house but couldn't sleep at all. Because the police couldn't establish intent, nothing happened to my dad, but I knew I needed to get out as soon as I could. A few months later I joined the Navy.

While Tim carried a duffle bag full of clothes with him to boot camp, he did not realize he was also loaded down with one of the most difficult, but most common, pieces of baggage. Although he may have tried to keep his baggage a secret from other people, he carried it nonetheless. The baggage Tim carried, the same baggage many, many people carry, greatly impacts our relationships, our marriage, our friendships, our emotional health, and even our physical health. This baggage is called the father wound.

THE ROLE OF THE FATHER IS ONE OF THE MOST POWERFUL, PROMINENT, AND FOUNDATIONAL ROLES IN OUR LIVES.

Fathers make an indelible imprint on the heart of every child. This will leave either a positive or negative imprint. The role of the father is one of the most powerful, prominent, and foundational roles in our lives. It is so powerful that a father can make an imprint on a heart even if someone grew up without ever knowing him. Each father determines whether the foundation he lays is a solid foundation or one that will crumble.

A solid father-foundation provides security and significance. As a result, a child grows up knowing they are loved, accepted, significant, and important. A byproduct of this foundation shows up in confidence, not needing to prove oneself all the time. A solid father-foundation leads to many positive traits such as being comfortable in your own skin, a willingness to take risks without the crippling fear of failure, and the ability to accept yourself just as God made you. All of this is fruit from growing up on a solid father-foundation.

However, when your father-foundation is a mess of rubble, you walk through life with insecurity, fear, and questions such as, *"Am I really loved? Am I really accepted? Am I really significant?"* When these subconscious questions gnaw on your soul, you will often travel through life with a wounded heart and an insatiable search for security and significance, often looking in the wrong place for it. Deep down, there is a genuine need and a longing for what essentially should come from our fathers.

If your father foundation is broken and in need of repair, keep reading. If you have deep wounds from what your father did or said to you, or did not do or say to you, keep reading. Even if your father has died, your Heavenly Father can give you freedom from your father wound baggage.

Powerful Prophetic Word

God speaks to the issue of the hearts of fathers and their children in Scripture. But the importance of words is determined not only by *what* is said but also *when* they are said. In regard to fathers and children, God illustrates both in the final two verses in the final book of the Old Testament:

> Look, I am sending you the prophet Elijah before the great and dreadful day of the Lord arrives. His preaching will *turn the hearts of the fathers to their children, and the hearts of children to their fathers*. Otherwise, I will come and strike the land with a curse. (Malachi 4:5-6 NLT, emphasis mine)

It is interesting that the final words of the Old Testament call for a prophet whose preaching will turn the hearts of fathers and children toward each other. And if this does not happen, their land will be cursed. There is something deeply significant about the relationship of a father to his children, and children toward their father. When a father and child are not facing each other in a healthy way, when their backs are turned to each other, when there is dysfunction, when hurt has separated them, the land in which they live is

THE REASON JESUS CAME TO EARTH WAS TO RECONCILE MANKIND TO OUR HEAVENLY FATHER.

cursed. Sadly, some of you know this all too well. This may describe the situation with your father. Your hearts were turned away from each other. As a result, you lived or are still living in a cursed land, in a cursed relationship.

The prophecy in Malachi of a coming Elijah was fulfilled in the New Testament by the forerunner of Christ, referred to as John the Baptist. If you are new to Bible study, John did not start the Baptist denomination. He was literally John the baptizer, John the dipper, John the dunker. When people repented of their sins, John baptized them in the Jordan River as an outward demonstration that the old had been washed away and the new had come. That is how John received his nickname.

To confirm that John was the prophet prophesized in Malachi, the gospel of Luke records the angel of the Lord telling John's parents what their son would do in the future:

> He will turn many Israelites to the Lord their God. He will be a man with the spirit and power of Elijah. He will prepare the people for the coming of the Lord. *He will turn the hearts of the fathers to their children* and will cause those who are rebellious to accept the wisdom of the godly. (Luke 1:16-17 NLT, emphasis mine)

After the little book of Malachi closes and before John is born, there are four hundred years of silence from God. There are no visions, no dreams, and no prophets from God. God is completely silent. I find interesting that the last words before four hundred years of silence is God's desire to turn the hearts of fathers and children toward each other. Then, the first words after four hundred years of silence is God telling us what the forerunner of Jesus will do: he is going to turn the hearts of the fathers toward their children. These two passages provide for us a glimpse into the heart of God. He desires earthly fathers and their children to be reconciled. In a bigger sense, the reason Jesus came to earth was to reconcile mankind to our Heavenly Father.

Magnetic Pull

I have always been fascinated with magnets and how smaller objects seem to be supernaturally drawn to them. As a boy I liked to line up little safety pins in a row on the table and then slowly slide a magnet parallel to them. One by one, the pins would begin to shake back and forth before flying toward the magnet and attaching themselves to it. Science tells us that magnetic and electrical fields are related, and magnetism, along with gravity and strong and weak atomic forces, is one of the four fundamental forces in the universe.

Another strong magnetic force is the one God designed between children and their fathers. Naturally, little children desire love and acceptance from their fathers. Whether in healthy or dysfunctional families, there is a strong desire to receive love and acceptance from our fathers, no matter the age or stage of life. Years ago, I met with a twenty-something young man in my office. When I asked him to describe his relationship with his father he put his head down and took a moment to gather his emotions, as my question seemed to hit a sensitive nerve. He finally lifted his head and said, "I have never once met my father. He has been in prison my entire life. But I desperately want to know him. I want to know if he loves me, if he cares for me, and if he approves of me. I really hope he does."

I see this magnetic pull from God between fathers and their children all the time. I know of countless stories of dysfunctional relationships between fathers and their children when, in spite of painful memories, the adult child is still trying to earn the favor and blessing of their father. When this significant foundational relationship is broken, God desires for it to be restored. God does not want your "land" to remain cursed because of your broken relationship with your father.

A Heart Turned Away
There are sound reasons that cause a heart of a child to turn away from their father. Although there are probably more, here are four ways a child's heart will turn away:

- **Disengagement.** When a father is disengaged, he communicates a lack of interest in his child. It communicates his job, hobbies, toys, or sports interests are more important than his child. Most of us instinctively know when someone or something is more important than we are. When fathers are disengaged, their kids will grow up with the feeling, *"I guess I'm not that important,"* and their hearts will turn away.

- **Demanding.** Having expectations and standards is a good thing. Demanding perfection is not. With reasonable expectations and standards, there is a chance to meet them. It is impossible to reach perfection. If a child believes he can never be good enough or can never please his father, eventually his heart will turn away.

- **Demeaning.** Comments like, *"You're fat. Why don't you lose some weight?"* *"I wish you were more like your brother,"* or *"Why are you so stupid?"* are demeaning and soul crushing, and will turn the heart of a child away from her father to avoid further pain.

- **Discouraging.** Proverbs 18:14 says, "The human heart can endure sickness, but a crushed spirit who can bear?"

Discouraging attitudes or comments communicate defeat and break the human heart. Eventually a heart will quit and will no longer have any courage to try. Discouraged children will turn from their fathers.

Likewise, there are things that children can do to wound the heart of their father. Things that can cause his heart to turn away are:

- **Disrespect.** The lifeblood of a man is respect. When there is a repeated pattern of disrespect from the child to his or her father, the male heart cannot handle this. Disrespect is a public but silent assassin for a man. Without respect, his heart will slowly turn away.

- **Lack of Appreciation.** A simple *"Thank you,"* or *"I appreciate this about you,"* goes a long way for the heart of a father. Without a word of thanks or appreciation now and then, a father's heart can become resentful or bitter. Over time, his heart can turn away from his children.

Moving Forward
If you have been carrying around the baggage of a father wound, there is hope. Regardless of the pain you have experienced from that man, whether he is still alive or not, it is possible to move forward with your life and experience lasting freedom from this heavy baggage. Let me warn you in advance, the following steps toward freedom are not easy and will go against deep seated, pent-up emotions that you may still have against your father. However, freedom beats bondage any day.

Step One: Attitude Adjustment.
To take the necessary steps toward freedom you must have the right attitude, or freedom from your father wound will continually slip through your fingers. You must take on the same attitude that Jesus had when He came to restore a broken relationship with mankind. Philippians 2 details the tone and tenor of Jesus' attitude: Jesus humbled Himself and took on the form of a servant in order to reconcile us to God.

The remaining steps towards freedom will require an attitude of humility on your part. Every fiber of your being might be screaming,

"No way! If anyone needs to humble themselves, it's him, for what he did to me!" I understand. But deep-seated bitterness will keep you in bondage. Jesus, of all people, did not deserve to humble Himself and take on the form of a servant. Instead, He chose to do this. Reconciliation leads to freedom. Reconciliation often requires humility.

Step Two: Choose to Forgive.
Reconciliation is all about forgiveness. It is impossible without it. In Colossians 2, this is what God did for us in order for us to be reconciled to Him.

> You were dead because of your sins and because your sinful nature was not yet cut away. Then God made you alive with Christ, for he forgave all our sins. He canceled the record of the charges against us and took it away by nailing it to the cross. (Colossians 2:13-14 NLT)

In order for us to be reconciled to God, our sins needed to be forgiven. This is exactly what God did for us. True forgiveness means that a debt has been cancelled. What was owed has been erased. As a result, we are now free from the weight of our sins. Reconciliation does not erase the past; it erases the debt that was owed. This is what God did for us, and this is what you need to do for your father.

You will likely say, *"But I don't feel like forgiving him."* This is bondage talking. You will never feel like forgiving; forgiveness is not a feeling. Forgiveness is a willful choice. Forgiveness is not determined by him.

YOU WILL NEVER FEEL LIKE FORGIVING; FORGIVENESS IS NOT A FEELING. FORGIVENESS IS A WILLFUL CHOICE.

Forgiveness is your choice to give as well as receive. Forgiveness is not condoning his actions and words that deeply hurt or wounded you. Forgiveness is choosing to cancel a debt that you are owed. Forgiveness is taking what was rightfully owed to you—to be loved, accepted, treated kindly, cared for, etc.—and writing DEBT IS CANCELLED on it. If you truly want to move forward, you must forgive him by cancelling the debt that was rightfully owed to you by your father. This will likely be the most difficult, but most important, step toward freedom from the father wound you will ever take.

After I taught through the issue of the father wound and the steps to freedom at a weekly men's gathering at our church, Tim stayed after the class and waited for everyone to leave so he could talk with me. His physical countenance was shaken. He had already told me about his abusive, drunken father and how much his father had hurt him. He had already told me how angry he still was toward his father. Tim had a great question: "How do I forgive my father who is no longer living?" This was my recommendation: Take some time to write a personal letter to your father. Write down what he did to hurt you, how this hurt affected you back then and even today. Then write your choice to forgive him, and why you are forgiving him.

Several weeks later, Tim let me know his forgiveness letter was finally finished. He explained how difficult it was to write, with the long-stuffed, painful memories that had returned, and the strong emotions that had surfaced. He then asked me if he could read the letter out loud at our next men's gathering.

The following week, I was nervous for Tim as he came up front to read his letter to his father in a room full of men, most of whom did not know his story. Tim spoke in the first person, as if his father was sitting in front of him. He calmly but emotionally told his dad about all the pain, rejection, and abuse he absorbed from

WHEN YOU FORGIVE YOUR FATHER, IN REALITY YOU ARE EXTENDING MERCY TO HIM BY REMOVING PUNISHMENT HE JUSTLY DESERVES.

him. He shared all the negative effects his father's abuse had had on his own life, career, and now as a father himself. After sharing all of his pain, Tim paused. Then he told his father that because of Jesus, he still loved him and that he was choosing to forgive him for all the pain he had caused.

When Tim was finished reading his letter to his father, it seemed like a mountain of anger, resentment, bitterness, and pain came rolling off Tim's shoulders. I witnessed a literal, physical change in my friend. The battle he had been waging was over and done, won by God's grace. Tim breathed in the fresh air of freedom that night, and he has been living in freedom ever since.

Step Three: Extend Mercy and Grace.
Many people confuse mercy and grace. Let me explain what these two beautiful and powerful words mean. *Mercy* is removing deserved punishment. *Grace* is giving unmerited blessings. When Jesus saves us, He extends His mercy by removing hell as our deserved destination. Also, when Jesus saves us, He gives us blessings such as forgiveness, friendship, hope, heaven, and many other gifts that we could never earn or will ever deserve.

When you forgive your father, you are extending mercy to him by removing punishment he justly deserves. Therefore, you must make the choice to stop punishing your father for his past sins against you. The past is the past. The past is over. The past has been forgiven and the present is about mercy. Extending the gift of mercy to your father is a choice to refuse bringing up the past and all the ways he failed you.

Extending mercy to the father who hurt or wounded you will be challenging, but extending grace to him might be even more difficult. You might extend grace to your father by giving him a place in your heart again, by inviting him to spend time with you, or inviting your father to build a relationship with your children. Understandably, how far you extend grace should be determined with how safe and healthy your father currently is. Forgiveness does not mean that you do not have boundaries, or that you must trust him. But forgiveness does mean extending him mercy and then taking steps in the direction of giving him grace.

Now, this may seem absolutely impossible. But with God's help, it is neither impossible nor too late. Even if you do not even know your father or know where he is, or even whether he is alive, it is never too late for the healing process to begin inside you. With God, it is never too late to begin the healing process between you and your father.

I have been blessed to witness real-life miracles when a person with a father wound chooses to forgive their father and then reaches out to extend mercy and grace to him. At first, they are terrified of being rejected again. But over time, I have seen God restore their relationship to a place of health that they have never experienced before.

I have witnessed miracles when a father, who has failed as a father, reaches out to his adult child and asks for forgiveness. Typically, his son or daughter rejects his initial request. Instead of quitting, the determined father pursues his adult child and communicates authentic sorrow for the hurt he caused. When the father is gently persistent, eventually forgiveness, healing, and restoration occurs. That is the powerful magnetic pull of the father toward his children at work.

But God
One of the best Bible verses that illustrates beauty from the ashes of pain is found in Genesis. "You intended to harm me, but God intended it for good to accomplish what is now being done, the saving of many lives" (Genesis 50:20).

These words come from Joseph, who is speaking to his brothers. When Joseph was a teenager, his older brothers acted out of hatred and selfishness and sold him into slavery. While Joseph was in Egypt, God sovereignly took him out of prison and slavery to become second-in-command to Pharaoh. Years later, Joseph's brothers traveled to Egypt to purchase grain in the midst of a generational famine. They were paralyzed with fear when they came face to face with their long-lost brother. Given Joseph's position of power in Egypt, his brothers surely thought their slave-turned-Secretary-of-State brother would kill them for what they had done to him. Instead, Joseph forgave them. In fact, years before their stressful reunion took place, Joseph had already forgiven them. As a result, Joseph could confidently and calmly say, *"You intended to harm me, but God intended it for good."*

The key phrase is *"but God."* Joseph was deeply hurt, but God healed his heart. Joseph was separated from his family for many years, but God orchestrated a sweet reunion. Joseph was in bondage, but God set him free.

Look at the steps Joseph took that gave him freedom from his bondage. Joseph *forgave* his brothers for all the hurt and pain they caused him. Then, Joseph *extended mercy* by not killing them for what they had done. Lastly, Joseph *extended grace* by giving them what they did not deserve: love, friendship, provision, and eventually a place to live.

With Freedom Comes Blessings

In January 2019, my mother moved two miles from my house. Four months later she began feeling ill, which revealed that cancer had been aggressively growing inside her body. My mother's therapies involved chemo treatments, major surgery, and more chemo treatments. This difficult chapter in her life allowed me to spend hours with her while driving her to and from appointments.

One day as we were driving home, she began sharing painful memories from her relationship with her father and how she had once carried around the father wound baggage. I only vaguely remembered my Grandpa Robinson, and what she shared with me were things I had never heard before. When I was seven years old, she had just given birth to my brother Bobby, and had to handle both of her parents going through cancer at the same time. She was close to her mother and spent a great deal of time with her in the hospital. However, my mom was distant toward her father and did not spend much time with him, although he was just down the hall in the same hospital. My mother kept telling her husband (my dad) that something must be wrong with her for feeling nothing towards her dying father.

When I asked my mother why, she told me that she had grown to hate him for how he treated her and her younger brother, Keith. I learned my grandfather often said mean and cruel things that broke the hearts of his children. While he thought he was being funny, he was in fact doing incredible damage to their relationship. As a result, my mother and my uncle developed a hateful and bitter relationship with their father. My mother told me that her hatred toward her father caused her to forget any good memories about her childhood. When her father died, she still felt nothing.

A while later, my mother came to realize her need to forgive her own father. As a fairly new believer in Jesus Christ, she surrendered in obedience and forgave her father for all the hurt and pain he had caused in her life and heart. To her surprise, shortly after my mother forgave her father, she began to recall many fond and happy memories with her family. It was like the fog of hatred dissipated to reveal joy, laughter, and happy memories once again. This blessing was God's way of setting my mother free from the baggage of her father wound.

I pray that God will set you free as well. May God give you the courage and the fortitude to forgive the man who has wounded you. Your father might have done much harm, *but God* can heal hearts and turn things around to accomplish many things for good.

Chapter Seven

Anxiety

In 2014 Geico made one of my all-time favorite commercials, called *Horror Movie*. I love this commercial because it completely mocks the stupid elements found in horror movies, which I hate. The commercial starts with the sound of a girl screaming, followed by a group of young adults running down a dirt path at night. One of the girls falls to the ground, and this dialogue ensues:

Young man 1: Come on!
Young man 2: Let's hide in the attic.
Young woman 1: No, in the basement.
Young woman 2: Why can't we just get in the running car?
Young man 1: Are you crazy? Let's hide behind the chainsaws.
Young woman 1: Smart.
Young woman 2: Yeah, okay.
Voice-over: If you are in a horror movie, you make poor decisions. It's what you do.

My favorite part of the commercial is when the guy wearing an old hockey mask in the shed turns around and takes off his mask, then shakes his head with a *"What a bunch of idiots!"* look on his face. The commercial ends with the group running away while someone yells, "Let's hide in the cemetery!"[9] Hilarious!

I hate horror movies for three reasons. Many involve elements of demonic activity. As a follower of Jesus, I believe it is unwise to open my mind to this. They also typically involve blood. I hate the sight of blood. Ugh! And of course, characters make predictable, foolish decisions. Thus, the comedic relief in the Geico commercial.

Horror movies are a metaphor for our next baggage topic that many people struggle with: *anxiety*. Every horror movie strategically plays on anxious feelings that are amplified with suspenseful music, darkness, moving shadows, and imaginations going wild about the bad thing that might happen next. Feeling anxious, worried, or stressed will lead you to make incredibly poor decisions. It's what you do.

Emotional Cousins

Fear and anxiety are often believed to be synonyms with similar symptoms. But they are not. Fear and anxiety are like cousins; they are different, although closely related. Both contain the thought of danger or the possibility of pain. They both make us narcissistically preoccupied with ourselves. In general, here is the difference: fear is a reaction to a specific, observable danger, while anxiety is an unfocused, objectless, future-oriented fear. Anxiety is an irrational, "what if" kind of worry.

What if _____ happens?
What if _____ doesn't happen?
What if they _____?
What if they don't _____?
And on and on it goes.

Anxiety is our body's natural response to stress. It is a feeling of worry or apprehension about what is about to come, or what may never come. For many people, anxiety is what they feel on the first day of school, going to a job interview, or giving a speech. It is that pit in the stomach after you read a text or email and begin to wonder what they are *really* saying. It is an emotional drop in your spirit when someone does not react the way you thought they would, or it is the loss of sleep while replaying a conversation gone wrong, twisting yourself into knots trying to figure out exactly what that "look" meant.

ANXIETY IS AN UNFOCUSED, OBJECTLESS, FUTURE-ORIENTED FEAR. ANXIETY IS AN IRRATIONAL, "WHAT IF" KIND OF WORRY.

A simple Google search for the physical symptoms of anxiety just might leave you stressed. Here are a few symptoms: stomach pain, nausea, headache, insomnia, fatigue, shortness of breath, increased heart rate, sweating, or shaking. But wait, there's more! If anxiety continues to run rampant inside you, your body will have what is called a *panic attack*. Some of the physical effects of a panic attack are intense heartbeat, whole body weakness, tight throat, random twitching of extremities, waking up drenched in sweat, and delusions about reality. This list is brutal. Your body is turning on its flashing red lights and loud siren to get your attention that you have an anxiety problem.

Anxiety grips us like nothing else, especially when we believe that apart from our best efforts, or in spite of them, something bad or unpleasant is going to happen and we can't stop it. Anxiety makes us believe that it is just a matter of time before the other shoe drops. Sometimes anxiety is rational. Oftentimes, it is irrational. No matter what kind it is, anxiety will have a negative effect on your health, as stated above. Not only will anxiety damage your physical body, but it will also negatively affect your quality of life and your relationships. If you are not careful, the baggage of anxiety can weigh down your life and mind into a life of bondage.

The Origin of Anxiety
Anxiety started with the fall of mankind. As soon as Adam and Eve disobeyed God and sinned, they hid. Hiding from God had never happened before. But that is what anxiety caused them to do. When God asked Adam and Eve if they had disobeyed the only rule in the garden, instead of asking for God's forgiveness they each started pointing fingers and blaming others.

ANXIETY WAS TRIGGERED BY SIN AND EVERY HUMAN BEING HAS BEEN EXPERIENCING ANXIETY, STRESS, AND WORRY EVER SINCE.

The fall of mankind in the Garden of Eden also triggered fright, panic, and terror between mankind and many in the animal world. Anxiety was triggered by sin and every human being has been experiencing anxiety, stress, and worry ever since.

One of my favorite subjects to teach on is heaven. Far too many people have a limited or twisted view of heaven. Studying Randy Alcorn's book, *Heaven*,[10] has had a profound impact on my life. Understanding what awaits believers in heaven has reduced my stress and anxiety while increasing my longing for heaven. I have often said the best part of heaven is not seeing Jesus or seeing my loved ones in heaven. *Can a pastor say that?* Yes. Because I believe the best part of heaven will be the absence of sin. Sin has devastated every area of our life, relationships, our physical bodies, and nature. Seeing Jesus in heaven, with the presence of sin, would trigger anxiety as well as being awkward and embarrassing. Forever hanging out with family and friends in heaven with the presence of sin would be exhausting and deflating. With sin, all of our problems and frustrations in this life would just continue into the next life. With sin, heaven would be no heaven at all.

However, without any trace of sin, heaven will be heavenly. Imagine having no anxiety, embarrassment or awkwardness in the presence of Jesus. Rather, imagine your time with Him always being exhilarating, enjoyable, and guilt-free. Imagine a forever with your family and friends, and never having any strife or stress. Imagine never facing rejection, disapproval, or worrying what people think of you. Imagine never being anxious when someone brings up your past failures, because without sin, no one will ever do that to you. Imagine every encounter with everyone in heaven being life-giving and incredibly refreshing. Imagine wild animals no longer being wild. Imagine having no natural disasters, plagues, or pandemics. There will be no sin in heaven and, with no sin, there will be nothing to be anxious about. With the absence of anxiety in heaven, you and I can live forever to its fullest.

In heaven, I just may take up sky diving. But in this life that will *never* happen, as I have always been anxious about heights. It is increasingly getting worse as I get older. Recently, my wife and I went on a drive and were told about a forest road that would take us to an incredible view of Mount Rainier. Without thinking it through, I took the forest road in my new 4x4 truck. This dirt road started out with a slight climb but soon began to climb steeply—very steeply. About two minutes up the mountain road, I found the courage to take a quick peek to my left. I saw an incredible, deathly drop-off. Thankfully, there were plenty of tall evergreen trees blocking my view to the canyon below. I began searching for a place to turn around. There was none.

My breathing started to strain, and my heart rate increased as we kept climbing higher. Sounding like a little boy, I started telling my wife, "This isn't good. I want to turn around." We could only continue forward and upward. Then came a sharp right switchback turn that literally took my breath away. There were no trees blocking the steep view below. It was a clear, corner cliff. My muscles locked up and I started to loudly moan, "I don't like this!" My truck was now moving at two miles per hour and drifting ever so slowly to my right—as far away from that death drop as possible. I could not drive faster because my right foot was frozen. Thankfully, just past the bend a blanket of trees blocked our view of the drop-off, and a mile up the mountain was a large turn-around opportunity which I used. But my anxiety was not over because I had to pass the corner of death once again on the way down. I literally began to pray that God would block any vehicle coming up around the bend which would force me to drive closer to the edge. Mercifully, there were no cars coming up the mountain. I eventually made it down the mountain to level ground, but the stress and strain caused by this anxiety affected me the rest of the day. This is how my own "horror movie" affected me.

The Bondage of Baggage

You may or may not be a follower of Jesus, but if you have been struggling with worry, angst, or apprehension for many years, you most likely have been carrying around the secret baggage of anxiety. You may resist hearing it referred to as a secret baggage. You actually may believe that your anxiety issues have been kept under wraps. But the truth is, those close to you have known about your baggage for a while. To them, it is not a secret. They have seen fear in your eyes, heard worry in your words, watched anxiety in your reactions, and experienced your stress through your excuses. Hopefully you have people in your life who care about you and want you to find freedom from your taunting enemy.

Before we talk about the path of freedom from anxiety, let's identify what kinds of worry you may wrestle with. I am not talking about anxiety or phobias involving spiders, snakes, heights, dogs, or the dark. If you are courageous enough to try, show the following list to someone you trust and ask them to identify any anxiety, worry, or stress they believe you struggle with. I have added several blanks for you to fill in if your struggles are not on this list:

- Anxious about failure
- Anxiety with success
- Worry of what people think of you
- Worry of inadequacy

- Anxiousness of loneliness
- Worry about death
- Worry of missing out
- Stress of rejection
- Stress of change
- Worry of being judged
- Stress of a lack of finances
- Anxious of losing control
- Anxious about the future
- Worry of _____
- Anxious about _____

Because Satan is the father of lies, he has twisted our understanding of anxiety in such a way that we often do not call it what it really is. We tend to assume it is just nervousness, concern, tension, or stomachaches. It is our way of putting Band-Aids on what we believe are harmless symptoms, instead of dealing with anxiety head-on.

Seeds of Anxiety
It is helpful to discover the seeds of your anxiety baggage in order to begin moving along the path of freedom. Discovering the seed of your anxiety is not to provide you with excuses or allow you to play the victim card. Rather, it is to better understand the reasons you have this baggage. Here are four different seeds of anxiety to consider.

1. Seeds of Our Upbringing
Our upbringing can greatly contribute to having secret baggage called anxiety. Maybe one or both of your parents were worrywarts. They were always stressed out and worrying about something, or everything. If so, you grew up with a culture of anxiety and your mind and body absorbed it. It is similar to what I wrote about in the chapter on Generational Sin. You caught what your parents were modeling for you: when in doubt, you freak out.

I grew up in a large home with both parents and six other siblings. There were foster kids and single adults who lived in our house, too. As a result, money was always tight. My amazing parents were hard workers who loved us kids, but they had to be incredibly creative every month to stretch the money in ways that other families with fewer mouths to feed did not have to. Thrift stores, hand-me-downs, cheap cereal, and bargain shopping were the rule for my family. My eyes were opened to the financial stress my parents faced when I was in junior high and needed basketball shoes for the new season. As a team, we all wanted to wear shoes that were the same brand and style. My father and I went to the Big 5 store in San Jose, and after a few minutes I met my dad at the counter carrying our team shoes. My father's expression changed when he saw the price tag. He said with a sad look on his face, "Barry, I really would love to buy these shoes for you. But I just can't afford them." I was the only player who played with a different, and much cheaper, pair of shoes than everyone else that season. It was not the typical teenage peer pressure that bothered me. It was the look on my dad's face that day. I felt I had embarrassed him by putting him in the difficult position of saying "no" to me.

A seed of financial anxiety was planted in my heart that day. It opened my senses to the pressure my parents faced on a daily basis. At the age of fourteen I started my first job and became, in many ways, financially independent from that point on. I began buying my own clothes, car, gas, and basketball shoes. The seed of anxiety grew some more when it came time to pay for college. Once again, my heart broke when my dad told me he wished he could help me but was unable to. I worked multiple jobs and saved like crazy in order put myself through college. At no time was I ever upset or disappointed in my parents for this. I knew they loved me, and I understood they were doing their best with what income they had, often going without so their kids could have food, shelter, and a good education. But I was unaware that the seeds of financial worry were becoming a secret baggage in my life.

When I became a husband and father, whenever there was little to no financial margin at the end of a month, I would lose my normal composure. I became short-tempered, irritable, and unpleasant to be around. My wife and my daughters used to think that I was upset at them, but they were never the source of my prickly attitude or actions. It was the result of the seeds of my upbringing. Once I became aware of the root of my anxiety, I was able to take steps toward becoming free of this baggage.

You may have had other experiences in your upbringing that planted seeds of anxiety into the fabric of your heart. Maybe you experienced ridicule from people close to you, which began a habit of avoiding taking risks or chances because of the anxiety that comes with failure.

Maybe you experience criticism as a child that planted seeds which eventually led to a paralyzing fear of what people think of you. Or maybe you were traumatized by close friends or family members dying when you were young, which planted the seeds of the angst of loss. Whatever your anxiety springs from, there is a decent chance that it took root in your upbringing.

2. Seeds of Secrecy

None of us enjoy being embarrassed or having our failures exposed publicly. On one hand, there is a healthy fear that comes with being held accountable. It motivates us to make wise choices. But on the other hand, knowing we will be held accountable for unwise choices causes some people to go to the other extreme: they hide their mistakes, hoping no one will notice. Anxiety grows exponentially in our concealing.

Keeping our sin a secret not only harms our conscience, but it also messes with our physical bodies. Our bodies were not designed to carry guilt. The physical results of anxiety described earlier in this chapter also apply to our bodies when we feel the constant stress of making sure what we have done does not become public knowledge. Concealing the underbelly of our sinful choices is exhausting. It requires constant monitoring. One cover-up lie will lead to another cover-up lie in an attempt to stay out of the fire. Eventually we struggle to remember whom we told what, and what we need to say the next time if or when we are questioned again.

PEOPLE EXPRESS INCREDIBLE RELIEF WHEN THEIR SECRET SIN IS FINALLY EXPOSED. IT IS ACTUALLY EASIER TO DEAL WITH THE FALLOUT THAN TO CONTINUE LIVING WITH THE STRESS OF BEING FOUND OUT.

Living with secrets increases the odds of our anxieties coming true. Fear of being found out can lead to all kinds of stupid choices, which in turn only increases our anxiety. However, secret sins will not remain secret. 1 Corinthians 4:5 says, "He [the Lord] will bring to light what is hidden in darkness." In Luke 12 Jesus said,

> There is nothing concealed that will not be disclosed, or hidden that will not be made known. What you have said in

the dark will be heard in the daylight, and what you have whispered in the ear in the inner rooms will be proclaimed from the roofs. (Luke 12:2-3)

The Bible says those who secretly conceal their sin actually intensify their guilt because they add hypocrisy to their secret. Hypocrisy is a grave sin in its own right. The only remedy for any kind of sin involves uncovering our guilt through sincere confession. I have heard people express incredible relief when their secret sin is finally exposed. It is actually easier to deal with the fallout than to continue living with the stress of being found out. That's right, there is freedom when we confess our long-hidden secrets. Stress subsides when truth is finally able to live in the sunlight.

3. The seeds of control
All of us, in one way or another, are control freaks. Some of us cover up our control tendencies pretty well. Other people could not hide their control issues if their life depended on it. You know those kinds of people. They want to control everything and everyone around them. It is almost laughable when they deny they have control problems.

Control freaks are exhausting people to be around. It's like their internal motor is always running hot, and their blood pressure constantly redlining, with all the worry and stress fumes they are exuding. Wanting to control everything will literally drive you crazy if you do not get help. But deep down, the real issue is not control; it is worry. It is being stressed about all the things you know you can't control or will never control.

Ask yourself this: Of all the things in your life, what do you truly have control over? The truth is, there is very little in life that we actually control. We can't control anyone in our family, can't control the weather, can't control the stock market, and can't control any politician. Nor can we control our boss, or the other drivers around us, or our neighbor, or the future. We have recently lived through a global pandemic and know we can't control those, either.

There is only one thing within our control. It is our response. That's right; when it comes to people, situations, or anything in life, we can only control how we respond. We can choose to respond with calm or chaos. We can choose to respond reverently, respectfully and resolutely, or we can respond in panic and paranoia. It is our choice. Those who have control issues are usually responding out of anxiety and worry.

In the middle of the quarantine during the COVID-19 crisis in 2020, I read some amazing quotes in the context of worry and control. Pastor Steven Furtick said, "Stop wasting today's energy by fighting tomorrow's battles! God's job is tomorrow—your job is today."[11] Lysa TerKeurst said, "Don't let your fears or worries of tomorrow steal your joy for today."[12] These are powerful, true statements.

4. Seeds of Anxiety

In our early, formative years, we are the most susceptible to having our hearts imprinted upon; these indentations can last a lifetime, for good or for harm. When young children have mostly positive interactions with family and friends, they can easily grow up with a tendency to trust people around them. However, when children face multiple instances of rejection at an early age, the seeds of anxiety could be implanted upon their hearts. These seeds could later produce a harvest of anxiety and worry whenever they face a situation where there is the possibility of rejection. They may instinctively avoid taking chances because subconsciously, they do not want to be rejected again.

WHEN IT COMES TO PEOPLE, SITUATIONS, OR ANYTHING IN LIFE, WE CAN ONLY CONTROL HOW WE RESPOND.

Our daughter, Holly, often experienced night frights at an early age. It broke our hearts when our little girl woke up crying, her small heart pounding hard. We would try to soothe Holly with prayers, songs, and bedtime stories. Slowly she would calm down and go back to sleep. This happened for years before we recognized the root cause of these night frights. Several hours after our family watched the Disney movie, *Anastasia*, Holly was fast asleep before waking up with another traumatized night fright. When she explained to us what was in her dream, it was similar to a scary scene in the movie we had just watched. We were typically careful in what we allowed our girls to watch on TV, but realized we needed to be even more diligent. The amazingly sensitive heart that God created inside of Holly needed additional protection. We even began to quickly change the channel that showed any movie preview with any scary aspects to them. When we did this, the night frights soon became a thing of the past. Even when Holly was in high school and we went to the theater as a family, she would still cover her eyes when a scary movie preview started playing. She continues to do this today, as an adult.

As parents, we can't always protect the sensitive hearts of our children. Candy and I realized years later the negative affect it had on Holly when, as a little girl, some of her "friends" did not show up for her birthday party. This planted a seed of rejection that wounded her young heart. Years later those seeds bore painful fruit.

The Antidote for Anxiety
I found the best antidote for my own anxiety in the little book of Philippians in the Bible. This antidote provides a choice to make, specific steps to take, the supernatural result that will follow, and a subtle reminder in the midst of my anxiety storm. While chained to prison guards, the Apostle Paul wrote:

> Rejoice in the Lord always. I will say it again: Rejoice! Let your gentleness be evident to all. The Lord is near. Do not be anxious about anything, but in every situation, by prayer and petition, with thanksgiving, present your requests to God. And the peace of God, which transcends all understanding, will guard your hearts and your minds in Christ Jesus. (Philippians 4:4-7)

The choice to make is a choice only a follower of Christ can make: choose joy. This choice is only possible if we understand the Lord is sovereign and has all things under His control. God's sovereignty reminds me that although the situation is out of my control, it is never out of my Savior's control. If I choose joy over worry, my gentleness will indeed be evident to all.

Verse six provides steps for me to take when I am anxious. However, the beginning of this verse sounds unrealistic: *"Do not be anxious about anything."* A better way to view this passage is, *"Do not* [stay] *anxious about anything."* To avoid remaining in a state of anxiety, Paul tells me to pray and petition. That is, I need to give every aspect of this stressful situation to God: tell Him what is going on, the emotions I am feeling, and the details of my fears, then ask God to help fix it, rescue me from it, or walk with me through it. But Paul adds this caveat: pray and petition "with thanksgiving." This spiritual stipulation forces me to look beyond the boundaries of the situation and express my thanks to God. I have found this added ingredient to my prayer and petition settles my heart, and helps me surrender this "bad" situation to a good God who has provided so many blessings in my life.

I have experienced the supernatural blessings of verse seven time and time again. The peace of God is hard to describe, but I know when I have it and when I do not. This supernatural peace truly transcends the little I do understand and goes far beyond all the things I do not. The peace of God rarely changes the circumstance, but it always changes me. How? It guards my heart from my emotions running wildly out of control. It also guards my mind from having all the *"what if"* questions rattling around in my head that cause sleepless nights and increased blood pressure. The peace of God is an absolute, priceless treasure from God.

There is a secret in this passage of Scripture that people often miss. This secret makes it easier to choose joy over worry. This secret makes it easier not to *stay* anxious. It is found in the words preceding verse six: *"The Lord is near."* These four little words remind me that I am not alone, that God is fully aware, and that God is right there waiting for me to reach out to Him. What comfort! What blessing! What power is at my disposal!

Going on Offense
Candy and I visited Holly and her husband, Luke, in the Denver area right before the coronavirus pandemic hit. We had a wonderful time together visiting some of the historic towns of the Colorado Gold Rush era, as well as several ski resorts in the Colorado Rockies. We even walked out to the middle of a frozen lake high up in the Rockies and enjoyed watching dune buggy races on the icy lake. Candy and I enjoyed the amazing beauty of Colorado and the even better company of our daughter and son-in-law. But one of the highlights of the trip for us was the surprise announcement that Holly and Luke were expecting their first child.

One of the other highlights for me was the meaningful conversation about what God was doing in Holly's life and heart. As parents, we had noticed a real change in Holly's strength, confidence, and maturity over the previous year. We also knew she had stopped using the anxiety medication that she had taken for years. Holly shared with us the deep-seated victory in her soul regarding her long-standing battle with anxiety. When she began to tear up while sharing, I instinctively reached for her hand. The more she shared, the more we all teared up. I was so honored and proud of Holly for sharing her story with us, a story we had been part of for so many years. I asked her if she would be willing to let me reveal what she told us in this chapter. Here is what she sent me when we returned home:

> Anxiety started at a young age for me. When I was very little, I remember having night terrors to the point where my parents came in to soothe me back to sleep. Sometimes I went to their bed for comfort. As the years went by, the night terrors slowly went away with prayer and protection from what I saw on TV.

> But anxiety comes in many forms and will continue to grow within you. During my senior year in high school, something broke inside my spirit. Panic attacks came flooding in with a vengeance as I was paralyzed by anxiety. Panic attacks were embarrassing as they often came at the worst of times. They came in public settings like during a school presentation, right before basketball practice, during a game, in the hallway, etc. I'm not exaggerating when I say I probably had about a hundred of them.

> The problem was that I hid the secret baggage of anxiety that had been building up inside of me for years. It didn't just happen when I turned eighteen. Anxiety slowly piled up like rocks in a backpack, until I could not carry that burden anymore. I was paralyzed and needed to go on anxiety medication.

> With the help of counseling and mentoring, I was able to learn some mindset shifts that helped me cope. But it wasn't until I learned who I am as a child of God that I gained my freedom. God is a good God; panic attacks are not from Him. Therefore, they are from Satan himself. He couldn't get me as

a little girl with night terrors anymore. So, he slowly built a stronghold in my mind to paralyze me.

Recently, I sensed a strong panic attack coming on. As I was beginning to cry and struggle for air, I stopped what I was doing and out loud, with the power of Jesus, I told Satan, "Get out of my mind, in the Name of Jesus! Get out of my house and leave! Never come back! You cannot touch me, for I am a child of God and you do not own my mind anymore!" As soon as I finished, I knew he fled. Instant peace surrounded me. I stopped crying, I stopped panicking, and I began to breathe easily. I then put on some worship music and sang out loud to refill my mind with praise to God.

For the first time I finally feel like I am on the offense in my life. I'm no longer playing defense, especially in my mind. For years I thought I just had to ride the wave when a panic attack came on and try to mitigate it. But this time I was able to stop it at its source, with divine power! I'm FREE! Not just from anxiety medication, but free in my spirit.

I want all of you to experience the power of the name of Jesus just like Holly has. She gained incredible strength when she began to grasp her role as a child of God. And because she is a child of God, she has direct access to His power. Satan is no match for the power of the name of Christ. In our own strength, we cannot defeat the giant of anxiety. We do not have the anxiety-defeating power that Christ has. However, we do have access to this power through the name of Jesus. David knew this and declared to Goliath, *"I come against you in the name of the Lord Almighty."* That is also why Holly boldly told Satan, *"Get out of my mind in the name of Jesus! Get out of my house and leave! Never come back! You cannot touch me, for I am a child of God."*

Let me close this chapter with a few words about worry from Jesus. Read them as if He has both of His hands on your shoulders and is looking directly into your eyes. "Look at the birds of the air; they do not sow or reap or store away in barns, and yet your heavenly Father feeds them. Are you not much more valuable than they? Can any one of you by worrying add a single hour to your life?" (Matthew 6: 26-27).

Chapter Eight

Fear

When I was a little boy, my father worked as a Deputy Detention Officer at the Santa Clara Boys Ranch, located just south of our home in San Jose, California. The boys who were sent there were rough teenagers, often gang members, who had committed serious crimes but were too young to be sent to prison. Instead, they would be sent out of the city to the Boys Ranch to serve their sentences with the hope that rehabilitation, counseling, and job training would alter the destructive direction of their lives and move them toward a more responsible, healthy direction for their adult future.

I remember my dad coming home from work with stories of breaking up fights, as well as chasing and catching runaways. One time, my dad was chasing an unsuspecting runaway and could see the path this runaway was taking. Seeing where the path was going, my dad cut across a field and hid underneath a log that the teenager was bound to walk on. Sure enough, the runaway came to the log and was halfway across it when my father jumped up and surprised him. Startled, the runaway froze, which gave my dad time to grab him. My dad was so good at hunting down runaways that word spread throughout the Ranch, "Don't run away when Mr. B is on duty!"

My dad took me to work with him from time to time. The first time I went to the Ranch I was filled with trepidation and fear as we drove onto the property and I saw the barbed wired fencing, security guards, and group of mean-looking teenagers. My fears began to subside while I watched my dad playing basketball with the kids. Those rough-looking juveniles laughed and smiled on the court when my dad talked smack with them. He also taunted those teenage players, daring them to try to block his left-handed hook shot. They never could.

Later that evening, as I sat in his office, I could hear my dad talking one-on-one with the boys, encouraging them with the potential he saw in them. I could see the genuine love my dad had for these troubled boys under his care. I also saw the looks of love and respect they had for my father.

However, one experience at the Ranch caused me never to want to return, no matter how much my father apologized and asked me to come to work with him. It was at the Boys Ranch Halloween party. I remember getting dressed up in my costume and enjoying the food that night, especially the desserts. But their Haunted House terrified me. To this day I cannot stand zombies, or people grabbing my feet in the dark or jumping out from the shadows to scare me. That was what happened in the haunted house that night. The worst part was a sight that is forever etched in my mind. I heard the shrill sound of someone screaming in pain, only to turn a corner to see a bloody scene where a "doctor" was chopping off the leg of his screaming "patient" with a machete. I later understood that it was all an illusion and no one was hurt. They had cut a hole into the table for the teenager's leg to slide down into, and the bone being whacked with the machete was a cow bone. But on that night, the pure fear I experienced paralyzed the boy I was then, causing me to bury my little head into my father's chest and scream as loudly as I could.

Experiencing one night of Halloween fear is one thing, but living with continual fear is another thing altogether. Most of the baggage topics in this book are secret baggage—baggage that we attempt to conceal or cover up. But the baggage of fear is unique. Many times our situation is known, and fear is obviously revealed on our faces and in our actions. Regardless, our fear baggage must be resolved in order from us to live in freedom.

As I said in the previous chapter, anxiety and fear are emotional cousins. They are relatively close, but also very different. Anxiety consumes you with worry over things that might, or might not, happen. However, events that are actually happening can paralyze you with fear.

The first two months of the COVID-19 pandemic in 2020 revealed how much fear gripped the hearts of so many people. A surge in respiratory deaths from an aggressive and contagious new virus that originated in China triggered fear throughout the world. This virus started a complete shutdown of our thriving economy as stores, malls, restaurants, churches, schools, and just about everything else shuttered their doors while our country quarantined itself. When people did leave their houses to purchase necessities, items such as frozen pizza, beer, flour, and toilet paper sold out, resulting in hoarding and panic.

Before the pandemic, the United States marked a fifty-year unemployment low in February, with just 3.5% of Americans unemployed. But a month later, the quarantine caused millions of people to lose their jobs, resulting in an unemployment rate of 14.7%, a level not seen since the Great Depression in the 1930s.[13] The major media outlets seemed to relish the dire news and rising death tolls. All of this produced great fear.

I know of a few people who seem unmoved by fear. They fearlessly stand their ground and refuse to run away. In the face of fear, they stare it down. They even wink and smile back at it. People like this are not paralyzed with fear, but this is incredibly rare.

Fear Must Fall
I mentioned Pastor Louie Giglio in the introduction of this book. I have never met Louie, but he has influenced my life and ministry through his books and sermons. He has also greatly influenced the kingdom of God with his Passion Conferences, where tens of thousands of college-age students around the world are challenged to surrender to Christ and follow him wholeheartedly. The Passion Conferences include moving worship led by Chris Tomlin, incredible stories of life-change, and then Louie powerfully teaches about the wonder and glory of who Jesus is.

From the outside looking in, Louie appeared healthy and fine. But many in the church world did not know Louie was suffering deeply, in secret. His emotions were spiraling down into a deep, dark cavern of depression, and only his closest friends and family members were aware of it. Thankfully, Louie aggressively sought counseling and medical attention. After several years of help, Louie regained a measure of health and freedom and is once again being used greatly at Passion City Church, his church in Atlanta, and the Passion

Conferences. However, Louie is still fighting his battle against what he calls his "giants," or what I am calling baggage.

In 2017, Louie shared part of his journey in his book, *Goliath Must Fall: Winning the Battle Against Your Giants*. He weaves in the famous Bible story of David facing and defeating Goliath. Louie challenges us to fix our eyes on the size of our God instead of the size of our giant, so it will not develop a stronghold in our life and end up demoralizing or defeating us. Louie discusses a number of "giants" people wrestle with, such as rejection, addiction, anger, and comfort. The first giant he discusses is the giant called *Fear*.[14] If fear is one of your giants, I highly recommend Louie's book as a resource for your health and victory over your baggage of fear.

A Relentless Giant

I agree with Louie that fear is a relentless giant. Like a zombie, fear keeps coming back at us again and again and again. In the biblical account of David and Goliath, the nine-foot-nine-inch giant from Gath kept taunting the solders of Israel. He did this morning after morning.

> Goliath stood and shouted to the ranks of Israel, "Why do you come out and line up for battle? Am I not a Philistine, and are you not the servants of Saul? Choose a man and have him come down to me. If he is able to fight and kill me, we will become your subjects; but if I overcome him and kill him, you will become our subjects and serve us." Then the Philistine said, "This day I defy the armies of Israel! Give me a man and let us fight each other." On hearing the Philistine's words, Saul and all the Israelites were dismayed and terrified. Whenever the Israelites saw the man, they all fled from him in great fear. (1 Samuel 17:8-11, 24)

I am not sure how you and I would have responded to seeing such a giant, but the fear felt by these battle-tested soldiers was real; so real they ran in fear to their tents. Fear does that to us. It causes us to freeze and then run away.

David, the teenage shepherd boy soon to become a giant-killer, arrived at the scene of this battle at the request of his father. He was sent there to give his brothers some Chick-fil-A and Lunchables and then return home with a battle report for his father. When David heard the taunting of Goliath and saw the solders sprint in fear to their tents, he was both appalled and offended. In his teenage exuberance and budding faith in Jehovah, David volunteered to fight Goliath. Following his interview and résumé review with King Saul, David headed off to fight for his God and country. When Goliath saw his teenage opponent walking toward him, it was his turn to be both appalled and offended.

FEAR IS A RELENTLESS GIANT. LIKE A ZOMBIE, FEAR KEEPS COMING BACK AT US AGAIN AND AGAIN AND AGAIN.

> He looked David over and saw that he was little more than a boy, glowing with health and handsome, and he despised him. He said to David, "Am I a dog, that you come at me with sticks?" And the Philistine cursed David by his gods. "Come here," he said, "and I'll give your flesh to the birds and the wild animals." (1 Samuel 17:42-44)

David's response to this giant is helpful for us in defeating our giants of fear. Read carefully, and take note of who David believed would give him the victory.

> David said to the Philistine, "You come against me with sword and spear and javelin, but I come against you in the name of the Lord Almighty, the God of the armies of Israel, whom you have defied. This day the Lord will deliver you into my hands, and I'll strike you down and cut off your head. This very day I will give the carcasses of the Philistine army to the birds and the wild animals, and the whole world will know that there is a God in Israel. All those gathered here will know that it is not by sword or spear that the Lord saves; for the battle is the Lord's, and he will give you into our hands." (1 Samuel 17:43-47)

Did you catch it? It is there for the world to see. David did not boldly declare to Goliath he was going to defeat him, but announced, *"The Lord will deliver you into my hands...for the battle is the Lord's."* What happened next does not make it into most Hollywood scripts: David ran toward Goliath. He did not move forward slowly, hiding behind trees or barriers, shaking with fear. David sprinted forward. How could David do this? I believe it is because of his great faith in the Lord Almighty and his confidence that God would be the one to defeat this giant, not him.

The key to defeating the giant of fear is faith. It is the only antidote to fear. You must believe that God is both willing and able to defeat the giant that has you in bondage. Only God can defeat the stronghold of fear that Satan has fortified in your life, heart, and mind. We have no power to defeat fear. Only God can do this.

Most people know how the story of David and Goliath ends. David threw one stone in the direction of Goliath and God guided it straight into the only unfortified part of Goliath's body, his forehead. One stone was all it took to fell this giant. He hit the ground with a dust-shaking thud and, after a moment of stunned silence, the armies of Israel raced toward the Philistine army, who then ran away in fear.

THE KEY TO DEFEATING THE GIANT OF FEAR IS FAITH. IT IS THE ONLY ANTIDOTE TO FEAR.

What David did next is a bit gruesome but a well-known art of war in that day: he cut off Goliath's head. David lifted Goliath's head up in the air as a declaration that this giant was never going to rise again.

Our Fear Story
In March of 2016, I noticed a change of color on the birthmark mole near my wife's left ear. Before we headed to Arizona to visit my brother and his wife, as well as soaking up some sun at some Spring Training baseball games, I asked our doctor friend from church, Mike, to take a look at her birthmark. As an expert in this field, he told us to visit his office after returning home from our trip so he could take a biopsy of it. After the biopsy, Mike assured us that there was probably nothing to worry about, but he wanted to send the sample in for examination just in case. Then it was Mike's turn to go to Arizona to visit his son. He told us he would let us know the results in a few weeks, after he returned home.

The following Wednesday, I started studying for the Sunday's message like I usually do. We were in a teaching series called *Life Apps* that had been planned out twelve months prior. But for some reason, I had no peace about the subject of the sermon plan. For an hour I wrestled with studying for the *Trust App*. Restless, I looked ahead at the plan and felt peace about switching to the next week's message concerning the *Encouragement App*. I actually came out of my office and told the staff, "For some reason, I am not supposed to preach about trust this week. So, I'm switching to encouragement instead." My study went smoothly the rest of the day. Teaching on the *Trust App* would have to wait another week.

On my drive home from work that day, my mind began thinking about trusting God. Strangely enough, I felt God giving me the Central Point for the message that I had postponed a week. I pulled into my driveway and thought how weird it was for God to clearly give me the Central Point for a message I was not supposed to preach on that weekend. Once I parked, I typed out the following Central Point in the notes feature on my phone: *"Our stress level is determined by the object of our trust."* As soon as I finished typing, my phone rang. It was Dr. Mike.

Mike asked if Candy and I were together, but I thought nothing of it. As soon as we were both on the phone, Mike got right to the point. "I'm so sorry to tell you this, but Candy, you have cancer. And it's serious." he said. We both sat there speechless. The word cancer hadn't even been on our radar. As Dr. Mike continued to share, he told us that he was still in Arizona but when his office called him with the results, he knew he could not wait to come home before he told us. We heard a quiver in his voice as he shared how concerned he was. He then said he would immediately set things in motion for Candy to have surgery in Seattle at the earliest possible opening to remove more flesh in the birthmark area and to see if the cancer had spread to her lymph nodes.

Over the course of several months, details would immerge that Dr. Mike chose to not tell us in the moment. We later heard that Mike's office staff began to cry when they read the specifics **OUR STRESS LEVEL IS DETERMINED** of Candy's cancer report. **BY THE OBJECT OF OUR TRUST.** Because it was so serious, they decided to call Mike on his vacation instead of waiting. Minutes before Candy's surgery, the surgeon in Seattle saw the detailed report for the first time. He immediately determined the depth of his cut needed to be much deeper. Her expected time in surgery changed from forty-five minutes to over three hours long. A year later, Candy and I attended the wedding of Dr. Mike's daughter, which I was honored to officiate. When he and his wife came to our table to thank us for being there, Mike teared up and told Candy, "Last year, I didn't think you would be alive to be here today. I'm so grateful to God that you are."

Needless to say, the initial news of cancer numbed both of us. That first night was difficult. Before we could tell a soul, we needed to quietly process the shock of what we heard. We did our best to pray before bed, but the giant of fear was alive and well in our bedroom that night. I could hear Candy softly crying in the dark. All the "what if" questions began to stir up fear in both of our hearts. I silently cried out to God, *"I need to hear from you tonight. I don't even know what to say to Candy to comfort her. I desperately need to hear from you right now!"* I sensed God telling me to go to Brooklyn Tabernacle's website and listen to one of Pastor Jim Cymbala's messages.[15] It had been many months since I had last heard one of Jim's messages. Once there, I found a recent message called, "Waiting and Trusting." That seemed appropriate, so I put on my headphones and listened. I knew right away that I had indeed heard from God that night in the dark. I also remembered the Central Point God had unexpectedly given me that day: *"Our stress level is determined by the object of our trust."*

Jim Cymbala's message was from 2 Chronicles 20, about King Jehoshaphat being surprised to hear the news that three enemy nations were on the march toward Jerusalem. Without the aid of radar or satellite imaging to provide advance warning, the king was told these armies were just around the bend and within a day's journey of the capital. He was shocked by this news. He had no time to rally his army to fight. He cried out to God and said, "We have no power to face this vast army that is attacking us. We do not know what to do but our eyes are on you" (2 Chronicles 20:12).

I sure could relate. I was shocked, and I did not know what to do, but I set my eyes firmly on the Lord as the object of my trust. The next part of the story was strange, but calming to my soul. God told the king: *I will fight this battle for you. Worship me and watch me work.* And God did just that for King Jehoshaphat. I felt God was telling me that His job was to fight for us, and that our job was to worship and watch Him. This allowed me to sleep soundly that night.

The next morning was a whirlwind. Our heads and minds spun as the Cancer Institute of Seattle called offering resources. We hung up the phone and the office from the surgeon called to confirm a surgery date. That was followed by another doctor's office calling to set up an immediate PET scan. In fewer than eighteen hours, our whole lives had turned upside down. When we could finally catch our breath, we listened to Jim Cymbala's message together. We held hands and cried as we listened. We sensed the same word from the Lord that King Jehoshaphat received: *God will fight this battle for us. Worship God and watch Him work.*

Even with a clear and calming word from God, the giant of fear invaded Candy's mind with questions such as, *"Will I be alive to attend Holly's wedding? Will I be able to see Kailey graduate from high school? Will I ever get the chance to see our future grandchildren?"* For me, I was weighed down with the fear of being a widower in my early fifties, losing my best friend and lover, and the dread of loneliness without her. Fear brought sleeplessness, tears, discouragement, and doubt. But that would soon change.

A few days later, Candy called me at the church. She told me her anxiety and fears were overwhelming her that morning, along with Satan harassing her while she was getting ready for the day. Then she remembered the 2 Chronicles passage about worship, so she went downstairs and turned on some worship music. She soon found herself singing loudly and even dancing with praise, her hands high in the air. Now, this is not like my wife. In fact, she had never ever worshiped like this before in her life. But as soon as she started worshipping God, her anxiety left. Her fear dissolved. The persistent attacks from Satan vanished. In their absence came joy and peace.

This became Candy's new reality. Whenever Satan attacked her with fear and anxiety, she started worshipping God. Every single time she did this, Satan left, taking his debilitating tools of fear and anxiety with him. Immediately, joy and peace would fill that void. This happened every single time. On several occasions, in the middle of the night Candy woke in tears from a bad dream. I would hear her putting on headphones and cranking up the worship music. The tears would stop. She would quietly sing and soon fall back asleep.

Candy and I were looking forward to attending our first *Thrive Conference* in Sacramento, CA, before all this took place. Everything was reserved and paid for. But when cancer invaded our lives, we were told we would not be able to attend. However, a week before the conference, Dr. Mike said the only way we could attend was if we drove. So, we drove. We were so glad we did; the conference sessions were encouraging, and the worship times were amazing. But on the last day of the conference I woke up at 5 AM, in the dark, to the sound of Candy crying on the other side of the room. When I asked her what was wrong, she told me that Satan had been especially relentless to her in the night and the fear and anxiety attacks were stronger than ever. We pulled out the laptop and turned up the volume on the worship songs we had grown to love on this journey. The same thing happened again. Fear and anxiety left and were replaced with joy and peace. Later that day, the surgeon called to tell us the great news that the cancer had not spread to her lymph nodes. It has been several years now, and the cancer has not returned.

The Soundtrack of Faith

Every great movie has a soundtrack. *Rocky. Star Wars. Miracle. The Avengers.* The soundtrack emphasizes what is happening in the movie. The music is soft during tender moments but intensifies when the action scenes come alive. If you watch a great movie minus the soundtrack, the movie may still have the same script and ending but will have a completely different feel. A great movie without a soundtrack underneath can actually be anticlimactic and boring. That is how powerful soundtracks are. I wish I had come up with the following quote but, once again, I must credit Louis Giglio for this amazing and true statement: "The antidote to fear is faith, and the soundtrack to faith is worship."[16]

THE ANTIDOTE TO FEAR IS FAITH, AND THE SOUNDTRACK TO FAITH IS WORSHIP.

Faith and Fear

Faith and fear are incompatible. Fear is faith in the opposite direction. Both faith and fear are belief systems. Both require a response based on what we regard as being true. A faith response is walking with my head held high because I believe I am a valuable child of God. A fear response is walking with my head down because I believe I am worthless. A faith response is believing God will deliver in times of trouble. A fear response is believing I must quickly take action and figure things out myself. A faith response is trusting God to bring me the right relationship at the right time. A fear response is jumping into an unhealthy relationship because I am afraid of being alone.

God knows us better than we know ourselves. He knows we have been fearful beings ever since the fateful bite of fruit in the Garden of Eden. This is why the most-mentioned command in the Bible is, "Do not fear." In fact, this command is given 366 times in Scripture. That is one "fear not" for each day of the year—

SATAN KNOWS THAT FEAR WILL SMOTHER THE ABUNDANT LIFE GOD DESIRES US TO LIVE. THAT IS WHY THE DEVIL LEVERAGES FEAR IN OUR LIVES AT EVERY POSSIBLE TURN.

including Leap Year. Plus, there are other directives from God's Word that include, "Do not be afraid," "Take heart," and "Take courage."

Satan knows what fear does to human beings. This is why he uses fear as one of his most effective weapons to defeat and discourage us. Satan knows that fear taunts us and harms us. He knows the destructive result of a slow but torturous drip of fear within our minds. He knows fear puts us in bondage and will eventually dominate every aspect of our lives. Satan also knows that fear will smother the abundant life God desires us to live. That is why the Devil leverages fear in our lives at every possible turn.

After being set free from the bondage of slavery in Egypt, the nation of Israel did not wander in the wilderness for forty years because they were lost and Moses didn't stop to ask for directions. In fact, God did not even stop them from entering the Promised Land. Their lack of faith did. Their fear of a few giants was greater than their faith in a miracle-working, Red Sea-parting God. A lack of faith and the baggage of fear stopped the entire nation in the sand and cost them forty years of wandering. That is what fear does to us: we wander in our own wilderness.

One of the most contrasting verses in Scripture is found in John 10. Jesus contrasts Satan's goals to the goals that He has for our lives. Jesus says, "The thief's purpose is to steal and kill and destroy. My purpose is to give them a rich and satisfying life" (John 10:10 NLT).

This is quite a contrast. Fear indeed steals, kills, and destroys. Fear ruins our relationships, our future, and our health. A quick Google search for the effects of fear on the human body is startling. Fear weakens our immune system, causes ulcers, damages our cardiovascular system, and causes people to develop irritable bowel syndrome. Fear even decreases fertility.

More people in the Western world are taking medication to sleep than the rest of the world takes in their lifetime. Some of the medication is prescription-based medicine, but other times it comes from a bottle of alcohol. This medication is often a Band-Aid for fear. It is to help us unwind, to relax, to forget for a short time the things we are worrying about. Simply put, fear accomplishes Satan's goal for our lives: bondage.

Louie Giglio says, "Fear chews away at our lives and erodes our sense of confidence and well-being. It robs us of sleep and rest. Fear binds us and steals our praise."[17]

Jesus promised a life without the bondage of fear. It is a life filled with joy, peace, and rest no matter what life throws at us. A life without fear is a life of freedom. It truly is a rich and satisfying life. This freedom can only come by following Jesus and keeping the focus of our hearts on Him. Faith is the only antidote for fear.

Freedom from Fear
Fear is the result of the fall of mankind in the Garden of Eden. Fear is one of the main tools Satan uses to put us, and then keep us, in bondage. Fear will cripple, paralyze, and defeat us like no other tool he has. However, Satan is no match for the power found in the name of Jesus and the power that praising God brings.

As an enemy of God, Satan hates the name of Jesus. But Scripture says that one day every knee will bend, and every tongue admit that Jesus Christ is Lord. That most likely includes the bended knee and confessing tongue of Satan himself. Oh, what a spectacle that will be! As an enemy of God, Satan cannot tolerate hearing the praises of God. When he does, he runs away, taking with him his handicapping tools of fear and anxiety.

On one hand, people often underestimate Satan's influence and power. Do not do that. He is a real entity who is at constant war with God and the people of God. On the other hand, some people give too much credence to Satan. They think he has supernatural powers on par with God. He does not; not even close. Satan can do many things, but he cannot read your mind. Only God can do that. So, when you silently pray or praise God, neither Satan nor his demons can hear those prayers or words of praise to God. That is why praying out loud in the name of Jesus and worshipping out loud to God is so effective and powerful. Satan and his evil minions cannot stay in the presence of someone who is serious about connecting with God in both prayer and praise.

SATAN AND HIS EVIL MINIONS CANNOT STAY IN THE PRESENCE OF SOMEONE WHO IS SERIOUS ABOUT CONNECTING WITH GOD IN BOTH PRAYER AND PRAISE.

So, when you are under the attack from the enemy of God, pray out loud in the name of Jesus, for there is no other name under heaven like His. Then, crank up the soundtrack of faith and give God praise, worship, and glory. Do it out loud, and do it loudly. Watch what happens. I am confident that using these two Satan-defeating tools will set you on a course of freedom from your baggage of fear like never before.

"For God has not given us a spirit of fear and timidity, but of power, love, and self-discipline" (2 Timothy 1:7 NLT). Indeed, the antidote to fear is faith and the soundtrack to faith is worship. Start asking God to increase your faith, and start praising Him!

Chapter Nine

Chain Breaker

Years ago, Stephen Arterburn was asked to speak at the chapel service of his alma mater, Baylor University. Stephen is the host of the number-one nationally syndicated Christian counseling talk show, *New Life Live!*, heard and watched by more than three million people each weekday. With a plethora of topics to choose from, Stephen felt compelled to share with the Baylor students his most memorable experience when he attended school there. He did not share about a fantastic finish at a football game, or a life-changing worship service, or a call to ministry during a missions emphasis week. What Stephen felt led to share was sure to shock those who heard him. Stephen told them that he came to the school to get a Christian education, but instead he impregnated a girl—and even paid for her to have an abortion.

What Stephen had done hit him with full force about three days later: he had destroyed the life of his own child. The disgrace of his secret baggage became a chain around Stephen's life. Satan used this to start a chain reaction of shame and guilt, causing him to believe that God could never use him and would probably never forgive him for what he had done. The guilt, shame, secrecy, and silence led to ulcers which put him in the hospital.

For many years, Stephen quietly carried this secret baggage around with him. When he married his wife, they soon discovered they were an infertile couple. They spent thousands of dollars trying different procedures to get pregnant. But each Mother's Day became harder than the Mother's Day before. Satan continued to leverage this baggage in such a way that Stephen believed every bad thing that happened in his life was the result of that abortion, and that he was getting what he deserved.

As God would have it, just as Stephen and his wife were on the verge of giving up, God brought a little girl into their life who needed adoption. Her parents were both sixteen years old, with no ability to support a child, and were looking for a Christian couple to raise their baby. In 1990, on Christmas Day, a darling little baby girl was placed into Stephen's arms.

God provided Stephen hope and healing against the lies of Satan. Romans 8:1 says, "Therefore, there is no condemnation for those who are in Christ Jesus." Not a little condemnation, but no condemnation. God does not carry it over our heads, waiting at any moment to drop judgment on us. In fact, when we become a child of God, Hebrews 8:12 says, "I will forgive their wickedness, and I will never again remember their sins" (NLT).

A few days after sharing his story at Baylor, Stephen received a phone call from the woman he had been involved with as a student. She told him that she had heard about him sharing his story—their story. Stephen tried to assure her that he shared in a way that protected her identity, and that he wanted the students to believe that he was responsible. What she said next was startling. "The next time you tell it," she said, "maybe you should be a little more honest." "What do you mean?" he asked. "Well, you didn't just pay for the abortion," she said. "You pressured me to have the abortion. You made sure I knew that you would not be there for me or for our baby that I wanted to bring into this world. You pressured and pressured. So I just did it because I didn't think I had a choice."

THE DECISIONS YOU MAKE TODAY WILL DETERMINE THE STORY YOU TELL TOMORROW.

Today, one of Stephen's aims in life is to share that every abortion involves at least one man. Too many times, the woman is left to carry the stigma of abortion by herself. Stephen is also highly involved in the pro-life movement in our country, telling both sides of this controversial and emotional issue. He tells his story, free from the secret baggage he carried for far too long. It is a story of hope and a future, with Jesus as his chain-breaker.[18]

Your Story
Do not remain in the past and play the victim card regarding your secret baggage. The past is the past, but you determine your future. Today is your day to change your tomorrow. The decisions you make today will determine the story you tell tomorrow. So, think about your answers to these following important questions:

In five to ten years, what is the story God wants you to tell? Will you tell a chain-breaking story of your family's generational sin cycle that was broken in your life? Will you share a story how the chain of enabling was broken because of some tough-love decisions you made? Will you tell a story about how you broke the chain to your abandonment baggage by fully embracing God's love and acceptance in your life? Will you tell a story of how God helped you break the chain of your father wound because you chose to forgive him as Christ has forgiven you? Will you tell a story of how you once were paralyzed by anxiety or fear, but that chain was broken when you tapped into the power in the name of Jesus and the soundtrack of faith? You are going to have a story to tell. The decisions you make today will determine the story you tell tomorrow.

What discipline does God want you to start? Nehemiah heard about the broken walls in Jerusalem and even traveled many miles to see for himself the embarrassing legacy his people were living in. But the hard work to remove the rubble and rebuild the walls did not happen all by itself. Nehemiah and the people had to determine they were finally fed up with living the way they had been living. Then they had to start the work. One piece of rubble at a time needed to be picked up and removed. Then, one limestone block at a time needed to be placed on top of another to rebuild the wall. They did not rebuild the wall by talking, reading, or even praying about it. They rebuilt the wall because they decided to start rebuilding.

What would your life look like if you started some spiritual disciplines of Bible reading and prayer? What if you started seeing a Christian counselor to work through deeper issues regarding your emotional health and secret baggage, even going when you do not feel like keeping your counseling appointment? What would your future look like if you decided to start rebuilding the walls of your life that have been damaged for far too long? The decisions you make today will determine the story you tell tomorrow.

What choices are you making that God wants you to stop? Maybe it is to stop believing your baggage is secret and you do not need to do anything about it. Maybe it is behaviors and habits that have chained you from living a life of freedom. What are the attitudes and faulty mindsets that need to be broken? You can choose to remain bitter, or you can choose to stop. Change it. Recover from it. Get over it. Maybe the chain that needs to be broken is that little poisonous phrase you keep repeating to yourself, *"But I just can't."*

You were designed by God to live a life of freedom. Freedom is never free, but Christ paid the ultimate price on the cross to make your freedom possible. He wants you to live an abundant life, but certain thoughts, habits, attitudes, and behaviors must stop to make this freedom a reality. The decisions you make today will determine the story you tell tomorrow. It is your choice.

The Ultimate Chain Breaker
As I have said throughout this book, having a personal relationship with God through Jesus Christ is the only way for any of us to gain freedom from our baggage. Jesus is the ultimate chain breaker. His death and resurrection broke the chain of sin, death, and the grave. Trusting in Christ as your Savior is your only hope in this life and eternal life beyond this life. Do you have a relationship with Jesus? I am not talking about going to church or growing up "religious." Religion will send more people to hell and eternal separation from God than anything else, because it gives people a false assurance that they are okay with a holy, righteous God. Believing there is a God is not enough, either. James 2:19 says, "You believe that there is one God. Good! Even the demons believe that—and shudder." Ouch.

Thankfully, Scripture is clear how to be saved from your sins and have assurance of a saving relationship with Christ, including all the benefits that go with that relationship. Romans 10 tells us clearly,

> If you declare with your mouth, "Jesus is Lord," and believe in your heart that God raised him from the dead, you will be saved. For it is with your heart that you believe and are justified, and it is with your mouth that you profess your faith and are saved. As Scripture says, "Anyone who believes in him will never be put to shame." (Romans 10:8-11)

The Bible tells us that when we are saved, we are rescued from the dominion of darkness and enter into the kingdom of God's light. It also says that old things have passed away and behold, all things are made new. That is some serious chain-breaking!

Anni's Story

I met Anni for the first time when she volunteered to pass out ice cream sandwiches at the end of a church gathering. I began to see Anni in the front row in the Sunday service she attended. I enjoyed watching her worship; it was as if no one was in the room but her and God. She often worshipped with her arms raised, or even jumping for joy. Other times she would fall to her knees and cry through the whole song. She sometimes shared my video sermons online, saying encouraging words about the message I spent hours preparing. What pastor would not remember and appreciate such a special person?

FREEDOM IS NEVER FREE, BUT CHRIST PAID THE ULTIMATE PRICE ON THE CROSS TO MAKE YOUR FREEDOM POSSIBLE.

The more I learned of Anni's story, the more it was obvious that she was carrying around loads of baggage from her past and present. Her baggage of abandonment and fear was burdensome and painful to her. It affected her marriage, family, and even her personal health in the form of eating disorders. She was trying so hard to look and feel good on the outside, but in her own strength, her efforts were exhausting and futile.

Anni finally came to the point of deciding to get serious with her faith in Christ after many years of "surface" Christianity. She chose to dive into her walk with Christ by digging into God's Word, praying beyond the obvious concerns, and making church attendance a priority. The results were obvious. You could see a positive change in her disposition and an obvious presence of joy in her life. Her husband and children started noticing a new Anni, mother, and wife. Her spiritual growth was inspirational and transformative as she found her identity and self-worth in her relationship with Jesus. It was absolutely beautiful to behold.

This transformation in Anni would be tested like never before when she felt a quiet sense from the Lord that her husband was not being faithful to her. When I first heard about this, I feared that she would take a big step backward in her faith. Instead, her faith launched her forward when the truth of infidelity came out. The new Anni did not panic, run, or get angry. She calmly forgave and loved her husband. When the two of them went into counseling, Anni remained calm and self-controlled in the midst of hurt and pain. She leaned into her relationship with Christ as she leaned toward her husband. At the end of one of the counseling sessions, her husband could not resist any longer and surrendered his heart and accepted Jesus Christ as his personal savior.

Here is a little bit of Anni's story, in her own words:

> My parents divorced when I was four but I was always close with my dad, staying with him on weekends and more often during school breaks. I was going to move in with him when I turned fourteen, but then he died before that could happen. I even wrote in my journal at that young age and said, "Now what?" He wasn't supposed to leave me. I felt so alone because my home situation with my mom and stepdad wasn't healthy. I carried a fear of abandonment so closely that I later realized I actually pushed people away, and then would pull back from them because I was afraid that if I didn't withdraw first, they would eventually leave on their own.

> It's been a pretty consistent cycle throughout my life. Those same fears and behavioral patterns continued to play out my whole life and even into my marriage. I used my fear to justify being controlling, because if I could control the people in my life, then maybe they wouldn't leave. But in the end, it just created emotional distance from the people I love.

> When my husband disclosed his infidelity to me, it forced a rock-bottom moment with my baggage. Through the course of counseling, I was able to recognize the origin of that fear and the behaviors that developed from it. When you're afraid to lose people, you tend to hold them so close

they can't breathe. Before either of you know it, something in the relationship has suffocated and the damage is done. I don't blame myself for my husband's behavior, but I can see my role in how our relationship got to a place that neither of us even recognized. Freedom only comes by surrendering to God.

I have come to recognize that HE alone is the Provider for all of my needs, including my emotional needs. He is the source of my identity; not human relationships, but my relationship with my Savior. Learning that my identity rightfully belongs in Him and not in any other relationship relieves the pressure on others to fill some space within me. God, however, will never abandon me because I belong to Him and He's promised to never leave me.

Many deep-seated chains have been broken in my life, but I am still a work in progress. I cling to Philippians 1:6 that says, "I am certain that God, who began the good work within you, will continue his work until it is finally finished on the day when Christ Jesus returns" (NLT). I believe fear of abandonment is probably my biggest weakness and the devil sees it as the chink in my armor, so to speak. When I begin to feel overwhelmed by those fears, afraid of people leaving my life, I remind myself that no matter who comes or goes, God is constant. He will never leave me. I cannot be separated from Him. "For I am sure that neither death nor life, nor angels nor rulers, nor things present nor things to come, nor powers, nor height nor depth, nor anything else in all creation, will be able to separate us from the love of God in Christ Jesus our Lord" (Romans 8:38-39 ESV). I believe the Apostle Paul is right, that nothing I can do at this point will separate me from God's love.

I live and pastor in a Navy town and am used to dear families being transferred out of our area. Though Anni has moved, we have been able to remain connected via Facebook. It has been a joy to see her continued growth in her relationship with Christ, and how His love has healed a fractured marriage. It is also a joy to see little children not burdened with the baggage their mother used to carry. Yes, Anni is still a work in progress, but aren't we all? I appreciate her authentic and transparent story being played out in front of her friends and family. The story she is now telling is of the choices she made to allow Christ to be a chain breaker in her life.

The decisions you make today will determine the story you tell tomorrow. It is your choice. Choose the Chain Breaker! Choose freedom, beginning today!

Acknowledgments

When I felt led to write another book but was unclear about which direction to go, God used Wendy Fox to remind me of the unique impact of the Secret Baggage teaching series. Thank you, Wendy, for speaking those encouraging words in the church office. God used your words to lead me in His direction.

God blessed me with an excellent editor to whom I am incredibly grateful. Thank you, Sharilyn Stachler, for sanding what I wrote to improve it and for encouraging me to expand this book with another chapter. It was a joy to work with you on this project.

Lastly, I want to thank my best friend and wife, Candy, for walking hand in hand with me through both the sunny days and the dark days of our journey through life together. Your love, faith, and encouragement are a priceless blessing to me.

About Overboard Ministries

Overboard Books is the publishing arm of Overboard Ministries, whose mission is based on Matthew 14. In that chapter we find the familiar story of Jesus walking on water while His disciples were in a boat. It was the middle of the night, the water was choppy and Jesus freaked out His followers who thought He was a ghost. When they realized it was Him, Peter asked to come out to Him on the water, and he actually walked on top of the water like Jesus.

But what truly captivates me is the thought of the other eleven disciples who remained in the boat. I've often wondered how many of them questioned that move in the years to come? How many of them wished they hadn't stayed in the boat but had instead gone overboard with Peter? Overboard Ministries aims to help Christians get out of the boat and live life out on the water with Christ. We hope and pray that each book published by Overboard Ministries will stir believers to jump overboard and live life all-out for God, full of joy and free from the regret of "I wish I had..."

What we do
Overboard Ministries emerged in the Spring of 2011 as an umbrella ministry for several concepts my wife and I were developing. One of those concepts was a book ministry that would help other Christian authors get published. I experienced a lot of frustration while passing my first manuscript around. I kept getting rejection letters that were kindly written, but each echoed the same sentiment: "We love this book. If you were already a published author, we would love to publish it." They were nice letters, but that didn't make the rejection any easier or the logic less frustrating.

Out of that came the audacious idea to start our own "publishing company." I put that in quotes because I want people to know a couple of things. First of all, we're not a traditional publishing company like most people envision when they hear the name. We don't have a printing press in our garage, and we don't have a marketing team. Basically, we're a middle-man who absorbs most of the cost of publishing in order to help you get published, while making sure the majority of profits end up in your pocket, not ours.

Our desire is to keep costs to a bare minimum for each author. (As of this writing, there is only a minimal contract fee when your manuscript is accepted.) We provide resources and ideas to help authors work on marketing, while also providing the editor and graphic design artist at our expense. We subcontract out the printing, which speeds up the time it takes to move from final draft to bound book. Since we don't have much overhead we can keep our expenses low, allowing seasoned authors, or first-time authors like me, the opportunity to profit from their writing.

Contact us
If you are interested in other books or learning about other authors from Overboard Books, please visit our website at www.overboardministries.com and click on the "Store" link. If you are an author interested in publishing with us, please visit our site and check out the "Authors" tab. There you will find a wealth of information that will help you understand the publishing process and how we might be a good fit for you. If we're not a fit for you, we'll gladly share anything we've learned that might be helpful to you as you pursue publishing through other means.

Thank you
Thanks for supporting our work and ministry. If you believe this book was helpful to you, tell someone about it! Or better yet, buy them a copy of their own! We completely depend on word-of-mouth grassroots marketing to help spread the word about Overboard Ministries and its publications. Please share our website with others and encourage them to purchase the materials that will help them live "overboard" lives for Christ.

May God bless you as you grab the side of boat, take a deep breath… and jump onto the sea!

Joe Castañeda
Founder, Overboard Ministries

End Notes

1 Merriam-Webster Dictionary. Web. https://www.merriam-webster.com/ dictionary/abandoned.

2 Spurgeon, Charles. *The Complete Works of C. H. Spurgeon, Volume 8: Sermons 427 to 486*. No. 477, "Never! Never! Never! Never! Never!" Delmarva Publications, Inc, 2013.

3 Abraham Maslow. (2020 October 11). Retrieved October 23, 2020.fromhttps:// en.wikipedia.org/wiki/Abraham_Maslow.

4 Agassi, Andre. *Open.* Knopf Publishing Group, 2009

5 Szalavitz, M. (2010, March 1). Touching Empathy. *Psychology Today.* Retrieved from https://www.psychologytoday.com/us/blog/born-love/201003/touching-empathy

6 Trudeau, Michelle. (September 20, 2010). Human Connections Start with a Friendly Touch. *CPR News, NPR Morning Edition.* Retrieved from www.npr.org/ templates/story/story.php? storyId=128795325#:~:text=Human%20Connections%20Start%20With%20A%20F riendly%20Touch%20A%20simple%2C%20supportive,and%20earn%20waitresses %20larger%20tips.

7 Smalley, Gary. *Change Your Heart, Change Your Life.* Thomas Nelson Inc, 2008.

8 Weber, Stu. *Tender Warrior.* Multnomah, 2006.

9 "Horror Movie." *Fandom: Geico Wiki.* October 19, 2020. Web. geicocarinsurance.fandom.com/wiki/Horror_Movie

10 Alcorn, Randy. Heaven. Tyndale Momentum, 2004.

[11] Cupp, Renee. "Sermon Notes: Pastor Steven Furtick – When God Says Stop." CuppFam.com, 22 March 2020, cuppfam.com/sermon-notes-when-god-says-stop/. Accessed 26 March 2020.

[12] Lysa TerKeurst. What are you having to trust God with right now? *Facebook*, 2 April 2016, 7:00 p.m., www.facebook.com/OfficialLysa/posts. Accessed 10 April 2020.

[13] Soucheray, Stephanie. *US job losses due to COVID-19 highest since Great Depression.* 8 May 2020. Web. 7 September 2020. www.cidrap.umn.edu/news-perspective/2020/05/us-job-losses-due-covid-19-highest-great-depression.

[14] Giglio, Louie. *Goliath Must Fall: Winning the Battle Against Your Giants.* Thomas Nelson, 2017.

[15] Cymbala, Jim. "Waiting and Trusting." The Brooklyn Tabernacle, May 11, 2010. www.brooklyntabernacle.org/media/sermons/20100511/waiting-and-trustinghttps://www.brooklyntabernacle.org/

[16] Giglio, p. 59.

[17] Giglio, p. 55.

[18] Arterburn, Stephen. (February 21, 2020). "Every Abortion Involves At least One Man." Focus on the Family. www.focusonthefamily.com/pro-life/stephen-arterburn-every-abortion-involves-at-least-one-man/

Made in USA - Kendallville, IN
87124_9781943635320
11 12 2021 0602

DEPARTING **BONDAGE**

ARRIVING **FREEDOM**

Every one of us has unresolved issues we carry around. In a word, it's called baggage. Although we do our best to ignore, conceal, or deny it, our baggage burdens our lives and negatively impacts our relationships. If not dealt with properly, our baggage can lead us to a place of bondage.

We often believe that our unresolved issues are our own little secrets, neatly tucked away from the view of others. However, to those who interact with us regularly or know us intimately, our baggage is no secret at all.

In *Secret Baggage*, Barry tackles some of the common types of baggage. This book is an excellent practical and biblical resource for those wanting freedom from their own baggage, as well as a resource for those wanting to help others gain freedom, hope, and a renewed future.

Barry Bandara is the current Lead Pastor at GracePoint Church in Bremerton, Washington. His best friend and wife, Candy, have been married since 1985. They have three adult daughters: Ashley, Holly, and Kailey. Barry and Candy are also a Papa and Nana to three beautiful grandkids. Outside of his family and church ministry, Barry is an avid sports fan who feels closer to Jesus when the day is sunny and warm.

Suggested Retail Price: $15

OVERBOARD
MINISTRIES

ISBN 9781943635320

90000

9 781943 635320